HALAKHIC POSITIONS *of* RABBI JOSEPH B. SOLOVEITCHIK

AHARON ZIEGLER

JASON ARONSON INC.
Northvale, New Jersey
Jerusalem

This book was set in 12 pt. Garamond by Alpha Graphics of Pittsfield, New Hampshire.

10 9 8 7 6 5 4 3 2 1

Library of Congress Cataloging-in-Publication Data

Ziegler, Aharon, 1932–
    Halakhic positions of Rabbi Joseph Soloveitchik / Aharon Ziegler.
        p. cm.
    Includes index.
    ISBN 0-7657-9978-2 (alk. paper)
    1. Soloveitchik, Joseph Dov—Contributions in Jewish law.
2. Jewish law. 3. Judaism—Customs and practices. 4. Judaism—
Liturgy. 5. Prayer—Judaism. I. Title.
BM755.S593Z54   1998
296.1'85—dc21   97–27111

Manufactured in the United States of America. Jason Aronson Inc. offers books and cassettes. For information and catalog write to Jason Aronson Inc., 230 Livingston Street, Northvale, New Jersey 07647.

HALAKHIC POSITIONS *of* RABBI JOSEPH B. SOLOVEITCHIK

CONTENTS

INTRODUCTION

The halakhic positions of Rabbi Joseph B. Soloveit-chik, zt"l, reflected in this book barely scratch the surface of the depth and breadth of the halakhic legacy that the Rav—as he was commonly known—has left with the world of modern Orthodox Judaism. The Rav was not necessarily known as a decisor, or *poseik*, of Halakha, but rather as an individual who had an uncanny ability to conceptualize the spirit of the Halakha on a universal level.

When I began attending the Rav's *shiurim* and lectures, my entire Torah learning and thinking was transformed unto a different dimension. For many years I was privileged to participate in his Torah lectures at Congregation Moriah in New York City, as well as his annual *Yarzheit Shiurim*, his *Teshuva Droshos*, and his exclusive summer *Yarchei Kallah* in Boston, conducted for members of the Rabbinical Council of America. In addition, I attended his regular *shiur* at Yeshiva Rabbeinu Yitzchok Elchonon—Yeshiva University—for one full year.

The sources of the Halakhos presented in this book come from my notes and tapes of the Rav's *shiurim*, as well as the *shiurim* of Rabbi Hershel Schachter, Rosh Kollel at Yeshiva University, who frequently quotes Rav Soloveitchik. Other sources include the book *Nefesh Harav* and the *Mesorah* publications of the Orthodox Union.

These halakhic positions of Rav Soloveitchik originated as a lecture series delivered at Congregation Agudath Achim/Boro Park West, where I have served as rabbi for the past thirty-five years. The *Jewish Press* subsequently printed many of them as a weekly feature, and as a result, I received many letters of acclaim from various segments of the Jewish community. I also receive countless requests for back issues of the *Jewish Press* articles.

In this book, I have attempted to formulate the Rav's halakhic concepts and written them in a manner suitable for the general public and for learning in the synagogue, school, and, most importantly, the Jewish home.

I am indeed grateful to my beloved wife, Libby, for her constant encouragement and patience in seeing the final publication of this book.

Rabbi Aharon Ziegler

Part I

Hilchos Shabbos

1

The Procedure of Lighting Candles Friday Night

The *Mechaber* in *Orach Chaim 263:4* states: "One should not light the Shabbos candles too early—while the day is still long—since it will not be noticeable that the candles are being lit in honor of Shabbos." The *Ramo* adds: ". . . and if the candles were lit while the day is still long, they should be extinguished and relit in honor of Shabbos." (*Tur*)

Rav Soloveitchik says that if the electric lights in our dining rooms are already lit when we are about to light the Shabbos candles, then we are confronted with a similar situation described by the *Ramo* (Technically, one could fulfill the mitzvah of candle lighting with electric lights. In fact, we do so in hospital situations—and with a *bracha*). Therefore, Rav Soloveitchik suggests that we first turn off the electric lights in the room, light the Shabbos candles, then turn on the electric lights and recite the *bracha*.

2

Facing the Door When Saying *Bo'ee V'Shalom*

When reciting the last paragraph of *Lecho Dodi*, our custom is to turn around, away from the *Aron Hakodesh*, and face the back of the shul. If the shul's entrance is in the back and opposite the *Aron Hakodesh*, and the *Aron Hakodesh* is facing east, everyone agrees that we turn toward the entrance, which is west, and say *Bo'ee V'Shalom*. However, if the *Aron Hakodesh* does not face east—prevalent in many shuls today—or if the entrance is not directly opposite the *Aron Hakodesh*, there is a difference of opinion as to where we should turn when saying *Bo'ee V'Shalom*.

According to Rav Moshe Feinstein, zt"l, we should face west and not face the door because the Shekhinah is in the west and it is the Shekhinah that we are welcoming when saying *Bo'ee V'Shalom* (*Orach Chaim 3:45*).

According to Rav Soloveitchik, we always face the door, regardless of where it is situated, because our turning symbolizes our welcoming of Shabbos, which symbolically enters through the door. Rav Soloveitchik used to walk toward the door and not merely face it, as was the custom of many *gedolim* in Europe.

Parenthetically, Rav Soloveitchik states that under the *chuppah*, a *Chosson* used to walk down the aisle to greet the *kallah*. This practice has been discontinued because, according to Halakha, a *chosson* and *kallah* today are not truly a *chosson* and *kallah* until after *kiddushin*. This practice was valid only prior to *Takkonas G'onim*, which combined *kiddushin* and *nissuin* into one ceremony. Before this *takkona*, when a *kallah* walked down the aisle for *nissuin*, she already had had *kiddushin* about twelve months before and was indeed a *kallah* according to Halakha.

3

Making Kiddush
on Grape Juice or Wine
That Is *Mevushal*

The *Rambam* states (*Hilchos Shabbos* 29:14) that for kiddush one should use only wine that is fit for altar libation (*l'nasech al hamizbeach*). This obviously precludes the usage of grape juice or wine that is *mevushal*. The *Shulchan Oruch* (*Orach Chaim* 272:8) rules in accordance with *Tosfos* and *Rosh*, who explain (*Bava Basra 97a*) that "wine fit for altar libation" excludes wine that is spoiled or has a bad odor. Therefore, grape juice or wine that is *mevushal* indeed can be used for kiddush.

The *Shulchan Oruch* further states (*Orach Chaim* 472:12), in the name of *Yerushalmi*, that one can fulfill the mitzvah of drinking the four cups at the Seder with wine that is *mevushal*. The *Rambam* presumably agrees. Apparently, he is stringent about the use of wine that is *mevushal* for kiddush, but not the four cups at the Seder.

Rav Soloveitchik personally conducted himself like the *Rambam* and avoided using grape juice for kiddush.

At the Seder, where the first cup of wine is the kiddush, those who follow the opinion of the *Rambam* do not use grape juice. However, a question arises concerning those who do not recite their own kiddush but are *yotzei* with the recitation of the *mekadesh*. The mitzvah of kiddush does not require the participating listener actually to drink, but the mitzvah of the four cups of wine does require one to drink. Must the first cup be non-*mevushal*? Or perhaps do we say that, because this is not kiddush but merely a mitzvah of *shtiya*, to drink even *mevushal* is permissible? Rav Soloveitchik felt that drinking the first cup is not merely a *kiyyum* of *shtiyah*, but also that of kiddush. Therefore, it should not be *mevushal*.

Note: This halakhic position of Rav Soloveitchik does not pertain to one who must drink grape juice for health reasons.

4

Yom Ha-shishi: Saying a Half *Posuk* at Kiddush

The *Ramo* states (*Orach Chaim* 271:10) that although the *minhag* is to sit while reciting kiddush, it is nonetheless proper to stand at the beginning because of our first words: *Yom Ha-shishi, Va-yechulu Hashamayim.* The first letter of each word spells the name of *Hashem*: Y-H-V-H.

The problem with this *minhag* is that the two words "*Yom Ha-shishi*" are the last words of a *posuk* in the Torah. *Chazal* tells us (*Taanis* 27b) that we are not permitted to divide a *posuk* differently than the way it is written in the Torah. Therefore, it is not appropriate to begin with the words *Yom Ha-shishi* alone, thereby dividing the *posuk.*

The *Mogen Giborim* writes that saying part of a *posuk* is prohibited only if we do not say a complete phrase. Hence, it is proper to begin with *Va'Yhee Erev Va'Yhee Voker, Yom Ha-shishi*, thus completing an entire phrase. The *Chasam Sofer* (*Teshuvos, Orach Chaim* 10) disagrees with the *Mogen Giborim*. He says that the entire *posuk*, beginning with *Va'Yaar Elokim*, should be said. However, the Midrash comments on certain words in this *posuk: Tov M'od* (And Hashem saw all that He created was "exceedingly good"), which refers to the concept of death. Because it is not appropriate to begin the Shabbos with a reference to death, omit the first half of the *posuk* altogether.

Rav Soloveitchik did not agree with the *Chasam Sofer*'s reasoning. He felt that the Halakha of not dividing a *posuk* must be adhered to. To avoid the problem the *Chasam Sofer* raised, Rav Soloveitchik suggests that we say the first words of the *posuk* in a low voice and then raise our voices at *Yom Ha-shishi*.

5

Uttering the Name of *Hashem* When Singing *Zemiros* on Shabbos

The *Ramo* (*Orach Chaim* 188:7) does not permit one who forgot to say *Ya-aleh V'Yavo* on Rosh Chodesh to include it in the *bracha HaTov V'Hamaitiv* and within the *Harachamons* because *Ya-aleh V'Yavo* has within it the *hazkoras Hashem*—the name of Hashem.

The *Mogen Avraham*, as quoted in the *Biur Halakha*, questions this stringency. In his opinion, the recitation of prayers, praises, and *tachanunim* is never prohibited, even though they contain the *hazkoras Hashem*. It is only prohibited when used in the form of a *bracha* and would be considered a *bracha l'vatala*.

Rav Soloveitchik agreed with the *Mogen Avraham* and did not object to expressing the name of Hashem when singing *zemiros*.

6

The Correct *HafTorah* for *Parshas Acharei-Mos*

When the *parshiyos* of *Acharei-Mos* and *Kedoshim* are read separately, the *HafTorah* for *Acharei-Mos* is *Ve'ato Ben Odom Ha'sishpot Ha'sishpot*, from *Yechezkel HaNovi*, who admonishes the people of *Yerushalayim* for their great sins.

According to Rav Soloveitchik, we should read the *HafTorah Haloh Kivnei Kushi'im* for both *Acharei-Mos* and *Kedoshim*, and never read *Ha'sishpot Ha'sishpot*. This custom of the *Vilna Gaon* is based on a *Gemara* (*Megillah 25b*) that states: *Hoda Es Yerushalayim Es To'aivosehoh* (Make known to *Yerushalayim* her abominations), *Nikroh Um'targaim* (is read and translated). According to Rabbi Eliezer, it is forbidden to read this portion as a *HafTorah*. There is a story of a man who was reading it before Rabbi Eliezer, who interrupted him, saying: "Before you explore the abominations of *Yerushalayim*, you should explore the abominations of your mother." After careful investigation, a blemish of descent was found in this individual's family history.

Rabbi Eliezer said that we may not publicly read a *HafTorah* that defames or condemns *Yerushalayim*. Although *Yechezkel HaNovi*'s statements were true, it is not our responsibility to repeat them.

A student once came to the *Netziv* and began to criticize the inhabitants of *Eretz Yisroel* for their lack of religious observance. Upon realizing what this student was doing, the *Netziv* immediately stopped him. The student exclaimed: "But, Rebbe, it is all true!" The *Netziv* responded: "*Hoda Es Yerushalayim Es To'aivosehoh* is also true because it appears in *Tanach*. Nevertheless, it should not be repeated."

Part II

Yom Tov and Holidays

1

The Proper Ending for the *Yom Tov Bracha* in Kiddush and *Shemonah Esrei*

Traditionally, we end the *Yom Tov bracha* in kiddush and *Shemonah Esrei* with the words *Mekadesh Yisroel V'hazmanim.*

Rav Boruch Epstein, author of *Torah Temima,* states in his *Sefer boruch she'omar* that this ending is an error that unfortunately appears in our siddur and *machzor* due to an original printer's mistake. Indeed, each individual *Yom Tov* should be mentioned by name at the end of this *bracha,* just as Rosh Hashana (*Mekadesh Yisroel V'Yom Hazikoron*) and Yom Kippur (*Mekadesh Yisroel V'Yom Hakippurim*) are mentioned by name. Sukkos (*Mekadesh Yisroel*

V'Chag Hasukkos), as well as *Chag Hamatzos* and *Chag Hashavuous*, should be mentioned during each respective *Yom Tov*.

Rav Soloveitchik vehemently disagreed with Rav Epstein. He believed that although Rosh Hashana and Yom Kippur have their own independent *kedushas HaYom*, thereby warranting their own *Hasimas Habracha*, the *Sholosh Regolim* emanate from one *kedusha* as one unit. Therefore, the single term *Hazmanim* is correct.

For this reason, Rav Soloveitchik also disagreed with the *Chofetz Chaim* in *Biur Halakha* (*Orach Chaim* 137:3), concerning a case where a *posuk* accidentally is left out of the *Yom Tov* Torah reading. If a *posuk* regarding Sukkos is omitted during Sukkos, then that entire portion has to be repeated. However, if the *posuk* regarding Pesach is omitted during the *Yom Tov* Sukkos, we do not have to repeat the Torah reading, the *Chofetz Chaim* rules. Rav Soloveitchik states that because the *Sholosh Regolim* have one *kedusha*, omission of any of them invalidates the entire Torah reading and all of it must be repeated.

2

Omitting Parts of *Lecho Dodi* on *Yom Tov* that Falls on Shabbos

Every Friday night we begin *Kabbolas* Shabbos with "*L'Chu N'ran'na.*" We say six chapters of *Tehillim*, corresponding to the six days of creation, an exclusive theme of Shabbos but not of *Yom Tov*. It is for this reason that they are omitted when *Yom Tov* falls on Shabbos.

There are different customs regarding the recital of *Lecho Dodi*, the beautiful and inspiring song written by Rabbi Shlomo Halevi Alkebetz of *Ts'fas* (*Safed*). *Nusach Ashkenaz* omits it entirely because it contains the phrase *P'nai Shabbos N'kabla*, appropriate just for Shabbos and not for *Yom Tov*. *Nusach S'fard* however, recites the first two stanzas and the last two stanzas, leaving out the middle five completely. This decision indeed seems strange. If it is inappropriate for *Yom Tov*, leave it out entirely. If it is not inappropriate, then why not recite the entire *Lecho Dodi*?

Rav Soloveitchik explains that the five middle stanzas refer to *Yerushalayim* (*Mikdash Melech Ir M'lucha*), the halakhic and political capital of our beloved homeland. On every *Yom Tov*, when we are required to be *Oleh Regel*—to be in the *Bais Hamikdosh* in *Yerushalayim*—we are deeply saddened by our inability to fulfill this lofty mitzvah because we are bereft of our *Bais Hamikdosh*. Our yearning and sorrow are so great that if we sing songs of praise to *Yerushalayim*, as we do in "*Lecho Dodi*," it would be like adding salt to our wounds. Because *Yom Tov* should be a time of happiness (*simcha*), the five stanzas referring to *Yerushalayim* therefore are omitted.

3

Giving an *Aliyah* on *Mincha* Yom Kippur to Someone Who Cannot Fast

Rabbi Akiva Eiger (*Teshuvos* 24) states that an individual who is sick and must eat on Yom Kippur can have an *aliyah* during the Torah reading of *Shacharis*. He is eating *b'hetair* and is not violating *kedushas HaYom*. However, this might not be the case regarding having an *aliyah* during the *Mincha* Torah reading on Yom Kippur.

Rav Soloveitchik analyzes this question as follows: Is the reason for the Torah reading at *Mincha* because of *kedushas HaYom*, as it is on Shabbos, or is it because of *Taanis Tzibbur*? Although a regular *Yom Tov* has no Torah reading at *Mincha*, Shabbos does. Yom Kippur has *kedusha* like Shabbos. *Tosfos* (*Shabbos* 24a) states that in the days of the *Gemorah*, there was even a *HafTorah* reading (from *K'suvim* instead of *N'viim*).

If the reason for the Torah reading is because of *kedushas HaYom*, then the *Mincha* Torah reading would be governed by the same rules as *Shacharis* and the aforementioned individual can have an *aliyah*. However, if the Torah reading is because of *Taanis Tzibbur*, then he cannot have an *aliyah*, as is the rule on every *Taanis Tzibbur*.

Rav Soloveitchik believed that Yom Kippur is considered a *Taanis Tzibbur* because we end the *Birkas HafTorah* with *Magen Dovid*, as opposed to *M'Kadesh Yisroel V'Yom Hakippurim* (*Ramo*, *Orach Chaim* 622:2), and the *nussach* for chanting the Torah reading (the "trupp") is the ordinary one and not the one used for *Shacharis* on Yom Kippur. Therefore, a sick individual who must eat on Yom Kippur cannot have an *aliyah* at *Mincha*.

4

Women Prostrating Themselves During *Mussaf* on Yom Kippur

The *Ramo* (*Orach Chaim* 621:4) states that our *minhag* today is to bow and prostrate ourselves when the *Shaliach Tzibbur* recites the *avodah* of *Mussaf*: *Lipol Al P'naihem K'she'omrim V'Hakohanim V'Ho'om*. We do this just as the *Kohanim* and the *B'nai Yisroel* did in the *Bais Hamikdosh*. We continue this tradition today as a *Zaicher L'Mikdosh*. The *Ramo* does not specify whether this *minhag* is meant for men exclusively or for women as well.

When Rav Soloveitchik was in Lithuania, he did not hear of women bowing and prostrating themselves during the *avodah* of *Mussaf*. However, when he came to Berlin, he saw that this *minhag* indeed was practiced in the *Ezras Nashim*. The Rav believed that this was wrong and discouraged women from continuing this tradition. He said that according to *Tosfos* (*Sotah* 40b), the *k'rovim* (those standing inside the *azara* of the *Bais Hamikdosh*) would prostrate themselves upon hearing the *Shem Ham'forash*, whereas the *rechokim* (those outside the confines of the *azara*) merely would respond with *Boruch Shem K'vod Malchuso* upon hearing the name of *Hashem*. *Hishtachaviya* (prostration) was required only in the *azara*. Our rabbis derived this practice from the mitzvah of *bikkurim* (the first fruits of the farmer's land). When the farmers brought their fruits to the *azara* of the *Bais Hamikdosh*, they were required to prostrate themselves, as the Torah states: *V'hishtachavisa Lifnei Hashem Elokecha* (*Devarim* 26:10).

During the *avoda* of Yom Kippur in the *Bais Hamikdosh*, women were outside the *azara*. Therefore, they were not required to prostrate themselves because there is no point in perpetuating a *zaicher l'mikdosh* for something that was never done.

5

Shaving on *Chol Hamoed*

In *Moed Katan* (13b) the *Mishna* permits haircutting during *Chol Hamoed* only if proper grooming prior to *Yom Tov* was impossible due to circumstances beyond one's control. The *Gemorah* explains that under normal circumstances haircutting is restricted on *Chol Hamoed*, for people might neglect to cut their hair before *Yom Tov* and will enter it with a neglected appearance (*Sh'lo Yikonsu L'regel K'she-hain M'nuvolim*). This expression implies that the prohibition of haircutting is rabbinic in origin. *Tosfos*, however, is of the opinion that haircutting is considered work, or *melacha*, on *Chol Hamoed*, hence biblical in origin.

Rabbeinu Tam, as quoted in the *Tur* (*Orach Chaim* 531), maintains that this prohibition is operative only if the hair has not been cut on *Erev Yom Tov*. He reasons that the basis for the *gezaira* is only because one "might enter the *Yom Tov* with a neglected appearance." This implies that one who has not been remiss in this respect is not restricted from haircutting on *Chol Hamoed*. The *Tur* objects to this reasoning and disagrees with *Rabbeinu Tam*.

The *Noda B'Yehuda* (Rabbi Yechezkel Landau, *Orach Chaim* 1:13) accepts the leniency of *Rabbeinu Tam* in a qualified manner: if the haircutting is done through the employment of a "needy barber." Rabbi Landau's ruling with regard to shaving gained wide acceptance in his own city, Prague. However, the *Chasam Sofer* disagreed with the *Noda B'Yehuda*.

Rav Moshe Feinstein (Iggros Moshe, *Orach Chaim* 1:163) says in our times almost all men who do not have beards shave daily and certainly shave on *Erev Yom Tov*. Therefore, the objections of the *Chasam Sofer* and the *Tur* do not apply. Rav Moshe also favors the lenient approach of *Rabbeinu Tam*. However, Rav Moshe permits shaving on *Chol Hamoed* only in cases of extreme need or great discomfort. He adds that no fault can be found with those who do so only for purposes of a neat appearance.

Rav Soloveitchik had a novel approach to this question. Those who shave daily are definitely permitted to do so on *Chol Hamoed*. You cannot do on *Chol Hamoed* what you could have done, or should have done, on *Erev Yom Tov*. The facial hair that you wish to remove on *Chol Hamoed* was not in existence on *Erev Yom Tov*. Hence, there was no negligence on your part and the *gezaira* need not be applied. Furthermore, the Rav firmly believed that under such circumstances, it is not merely permissible to shave, but a mitzvah to do so, in order not to have a "neglected appearance" (a state of *menuvol*) on *Chol Hamoed* or for the last days of *Yom Tov*.

6

Problems with Reading the *Megillah* on Shabbos *Chol Hamoed*

The *Ramo* (*Orach Chaim* 490:9 and 663:2) states that it is our *minhag* to read *Megillas Koheles* on Shabbos *Chol Hamoed* Sukkos and *Megillas Shir Ha-Shirim* on Shabbos *Chol Hamoed* Pesach.

A serious question arises: how could such a *minhag* have been instituted when *Chazal* prohibit us from reading any parts of *K'ssuvim* on Shabbos (*Mishna* in *Shabbos* 115a: *U'mipnei Ma Ain Kor'im Bo'hem? Mipnei Bittul Bais HaMidrash*) (Why do we not read them (*K'ssuvim*)? Because of the neglect of the *Bais HaMidrash*.) Rashi explains that *Chazal* were afraid that people would become so engrossed in the exciting stories in *K'ssuvim* that they would miss the *Rov*'s Shabbos Torah *shiur*. *Chazal* felt this *shiur* was too important, so they banned the reading of *K'ssuvim* both privately and publicly.

Rav Soloveitchik felt that the ban on *K'ssuvim* only applied during the hours that the *Rov* gave his *shiur*, which was after *Krias HaTorah* of *Shacharis* and until *Krias HaTorah* of *Mincha*. However, the ban did not apply before or after this time span. Therefore, the *Megillah* readings of Shabbos *Chol Hamoed* were set specifically before the regular Torah reading of *Shacharis*.

Another problem we encounter is the *gezaira* of *Rabbah*, which prohibits taking the *Shofar*, *Lulav*, and *Megillah* on Shabbos because we might come to carry them and thus violate the *issur* Shabbos (*Rosh HaShono* 29a). Why, then, on Shabbos are we permitted to read *Megillas Koheles*, *Shir HaShirim*, and *Rus*, yet prohibited to read *Megillas Esther*?

Rav Soloveitchik responds to this quandary by citing the *Vilna Gaon*, who noted that the *gezaira* of *Rabbah* only applied when there was an obligation on each individual. However, when there is an obligation on the *tzibbur* as a whole, but not on each individual, we are not afraid that one will forget himself and carry a needed item in the *Reshus HoRabim*. Because the reading of *Kohelles* and *Shir Hashirim* is incumbent upon the *tzibbur* as a whole but not on each individual, they may be read on Shabbos, just as the Torah is read on Shabbos.

7

Eating in the Sukkah on *Shemini Atzeres*

According to the Halakha, in *Chutz L'aretz*, we are required to eat in the sukkah the night of *Shemini Atzeres* as well as all day, albeit without saying the *bracha "Leshev Ba'Sukkah"* (*Orach Chaim* 668:1).

Just as we extend the *Yom Tov* of Pesach one day (in *Chutz L'aretz*) and are prohibited to eat *Chometz* because it is *Yom Tov Sheni Shel Goliyos* (according to rabbinic law), so too are we required to extend the *Yom Tov* of Sukkos one day as a *Yom Tov Sheni Shel Goliyos* and eat our meals in the sukkah. The only difference between Sukkos and Pesach is that on Pesach there is no problem with the rabbis extending the *Yom Tov* one day; however, on Sukkos we do indeed have a problem. The Torah has designated the day following the seventh day of Sukkos as a special *Yom Tov*, or *Shemini Atzeres*. The *Gemorah* declares this day as an independent *Yom Tov* regarding six specific Halakhos, with the acronym of P-Z-R-K-SH-B (*Sukkah 48a*).

To resolve this dilemma, the *Gemorah* ruled that "*MISAV YASVINON, B'RUCHEI LO M'VOR'CHINON*" (we are required to sit in the sukkah, but without a *bracha* (*Sukkah 47a*).

In spite of this ruling, which the *Rambam* and *Shulchan Oruch* duly codified in the Halakha, there exists a popular *minhag* that we not eat in the sukkah on *Shemini Atzeres*. This *minhag*, though contrary to basic Halakha, nevertheless has the support of many great *tzaddikim* and *Talmidei chachomim*. This paradox is mind-boggling; how can a *minhag* that defies all halakhic principles be so widely accepted?

According to Rav Soloveitchik, this *minhag* stems from the founders of the hasidic movement, who had a great love and yearning for *Eretz Yisroel*. Their intention was to demonstrate solidarity with the people of *Eretz Yisroel* by totally identifying one day with them. In *Eretz Yisroel*, obviously, there is no eighth day Pesach and no eighth day Sukkos as a *Yom Tov Sheni*. *Shemini Atzeres* is a completely independent *Yom Tov* from Sukkos, and one certainly does not eat in the sukkah. Therefore, the great Hasidic rabbis wanted to build a bridge of love between the communities of *Eretz Yisroel* and the Diaspora by observing this one day of *Shemini Atzeres* in *Chutz L'aretz* exactly as it is being observed in *Eretz Yisroel.*

Although the Rav himself always ate in his sukkah on *Shemini Atzeres,* he often said that he could not criticize those who did not and that he even could empathize with them.

8

Pregnant Women Eating the *Esrog* After Sukkos

There is a prevalent custom among pregnant women to eat from the *esrog* after Sukkos. The *Mateh Efrayim* even prints a special *Y'HI RATZON* for them to recite while they eat it. However, the *Mateh Efrayim* offers no sources for this *minhag* and many *poskim* have questioned its validity.

According to Rav Soloveitchik, this *minhag* has great merit and authenticity. The *Gemorah* (*Sanhedrin* 70a) discusses the kind of tree the *Eitz Ha-Daas* was, and the *Midrash* (*Braishis Rabba* 20) declares the forbidden fruit to have been from an *esrog* tree. The Rav noted that the Christians always believed it was an apple tree because of their misinterpretation of the word *tapuach*, which *Tosfos* uses to refer to citrus fruit (*Taanis* 30a). Indeed, in modern Hebrew, *tapuach* means apple, but in talmudic days people didn't have apples or even know of them.

Rav Soloveitchik suggests that because the pain and suffering of women in childbirth stem from the eating of *Eitz Ha-Daas* (*B'etzev Taildi Bonim, Braishis* 3:16), the woman solemnly declares in her *Y'hi Ratzon* prayer to *Hashem* that, had she been there, she would not have eaten of the forbidden fruit. According to the Midrash, the *Eitz Ha-Daas* was only forbidden before Shabbos and would have been permitted right after it. But Chava was not able to control herself and therefore was punished. The Rav concluded that the pregnant woman now states: "You see, *Hashem*, I had an *esrog* in my hands all of *Yom Tov* Sukkos, yet I controlled my temptation and didn't eat of it until after Sukkos. Likewise, had I been there, I would have waited until after Shabbos. I therefore plead that You will hear my cry and mitigate my pain and suffering."

9

Celebrating Thanksgiving
and Eating Turkey

The Torah states (*Va-Yik'ra 18:3*): *U'vechukosaihem Lo Sailaichu* (And do not follow their traditions). This edict is discussed in the *Gemara* (*Avoda Zara* 11a), and *Tosfos* concludes that two distinct types of customs are forbidden. The first are idolatrous, and the second are foolish ones found in the Gentile community, even if their origins are *not* idolatrous. The *Ran* disagrees and rules that only customs with a basis in idolatrous practice are prohibited. The *Ramo* (*Yorah Deah* 178:1) agrees with the *Ran*, stating: "Any custom done out of honor or any other reason is permissible, as long as there is no taint of idolatrous origin." (The *Vilna Gaon* disagreed with the *Ramo* and ruled that the only time "secular" customs are permissible is when they have a "Jewish" origin.)

Rabbi Yitzchak Hutner (*Pachad Yitzchok*, p. 109) appears to have adapted a stringent view on this matter. He writes that the establishment of an annual holiday based on the Christian calendar is associated with idol worship and thus prohibited. Rabbi Menashe Klein (*Mishne Halachos* 10:116) concurs with this prohibition.

Rabbi Yehuda Henkin (*Teshuvos B'nei Banim* 2:30) felt that this is an unnecessary prohibition and that Halakha does *not* consider Thanksgiving a religious holiday. Rav Moshe Feinstein (*Iggros Moshe, Even HaEzer* 3:13) states that Thanksgiving is not a religious holiday and Halakha therefore does not prohibit its observance. However, he adds that *ba'alei nefesh* (pious people) should be strict regarding the matter.

According to Rav Soloveitchik, Thanksgiving is not regarded as a Gentile holiday and it is permissible to eat turkey on this day (*Nefesh Harav*, p. 231). He felt there was no problem with the kashrus of turkey, an opinion shared by his father, Rabbi Moshe Soloveitchik. Indeed, Rav Soloveitchik implied to his students that he and his family celebrated Thanksgiving, though he never canceled his *shiur* on that day.

10

Lighting Hanukkah Candles Before *Havdalah* in *Shul*

Many authorities, including the *Rambam*, say that *Havdalah* at the conclusion of Shabbos is a biblical requirement and that no *melacha* (work) should be undertaken on *Mo'tzoei* Shabbos until *Havdalah* has been recited or heard. Therefore, it seems quite strange that the *Shulchon Oruch* should state (*Orach Chaim* 681:2) that on *Mo'tzoei* Shabbos we are to kindle the Hanukkah candles in the synagogue *before Havdalah*. Furthermore, the *Ramo* adds that one *definitely* should follow this procedure at home.

The *Mishneh B'rurah* quotes many authorities (note 3), including the *Taz*, who disagree with the basic principle of the *Mechaber* and maintain that

Havdalah must precede ner Hanukkah at all times. Our *minhag* is that in the synagogue we follow the *Mechaber* (first *ner* Hanukkah and then *Havdalah*), while at home we follow the *Taz* (reciting *Havdalah* before *ner* Hanukkah).

According to Rav Soloveitchik, the *mechaber*'s rationale is quite logical and based on an important principle. The *Vilna Gaon* states (671:21) that the purpose of lighting *ner* Hanukkah in the synagogue, (though no one fulfills their personal requirement that way), is because of *Pirsumai Nissa* (publicly acknowledging the miracle that *Hashem* wrought). Whenever an individual is required to perform the mitzvah of *Pirsumai Nissa*, it is incumbent upon him to do so publicly, in the synagogue. He derives this concept from the original requirement of saying *hallel* at the Seder of Pesach, a requirement that later was extended to recitation in the synagogue, as a *minhag*, during *Ma'ariv*. The same applies for *ner Hanukkah*. With this premise, the Rav explains, we readily can understand the *M'chaber*.

The performance of *Pirsumai Nissa* in the shul can be fulfilled only when we have a *halakhic tzibbur* present—a quorum of ten or more male adults to act as a functioning *tzibbur* in terms of *tefillah* or Torah reading. As long as davening is not over, the need for a *tzibbur* exists. Once davening has ended, the need for a functioning *tzibbur* ceases.

The fact that many people are still present does not unite them into a halakhic *tzibbur*; they are regarded as a large group of people who are together, but for no halakhic purpose. Hence, Rav Soloveitchik reasons, once *Havdalah* is recited, it is a signal that *Tefillah* has ended and a halakhic *tzibbur* no longer exists. In order for *ner* Hanukkah to have the effect of *Pirsumai Nissa*, it must be lit before *Havdalah*.

The *minhag* of Reb Chaim Soloveitchik in Brisk was to light the *ner* Hanukkah even before the recital of *Ve'hi No'am* so that we have a positive halakhic *tzibbur* presence, for he felt that once kaddish with *Tis'kabel* was recited, the need for *Tefillah B'tzibbur* was over.

11

The *Bracha* of *She'asa Nissim* as a *Birchas* Mitzvah

The *Ramo* (*Orach Chaim* 676:2) states that we are to recite both *brachos*, *L'hadlik Ner* and *She'asa Nissim*, before we perform the actual mitzvah of lighting the candle. The *Mishna B'rura* notes that the reason for this is that we must say the *brachos*— *Ohvair La'a'siyoson*—as close to the performance of the mitzvah as possible.

This is, of course, true of every *birchas* mitzvah —that we are to do it *Ohvair La'a'siyoson*. What is unusual in this case is that the *Ramo* includes the second *bracha* (*She'asa Nissim*) in this arrangement, when indeed the second *bracha* is *not* a *birchas* mitzvah, but rather a *birchas shevach*. It would have seemed more logical to light the candle immediately following the *birchas* mitzvah (*L'hadlik ner*), recite the *She'asa Nissim* after the candle lighting, and not interfere with the *Ohvair La'a'siyoson* between the first *bracha* and the actual mitzvah.

Rav Soloveitchik noted that the *Gemorah* (*Shabbos* 21b) begins by asking: *Mai Hanukkah?* (Why did our sages institute the mitzvah of *Hanukkah?*) And the Talmud relates the events of the twenty-fifth day of *Kislev* and the miracle that followed. The *Gemorah* then continues (22a) with what seems a most unrelated statement: that a *ner Hanukkah* placed above the height of twenty *ammos* is invalid for the mitzvah, just as a sukkah with a *s'chach* more than twenty *ammos* or a *mo'vui* (an alley) with a crossbeam over the entrance higher than twenty *ammos* become unfit. The Rav asked what connection the *Gemorah* was trying to make between the historical events of *Hanukkah* and the Halakhos of sukkah. It seemed to him that the *Gemorah* was teaching us that one does not fulfill the mitzvah of sukkah by simply reciting the *bracha* and eating in the sukkah *without being aware of the reason for doing so.* Ordinarily, the lack of awareness as to the reason behind a mitzvah does not hinder its efficacy because the Torah in most instances does not reveal the reasons to us. However, because in the case of sukkah the Torah goes out of its way to state the reason for our dwelling in it—*Ki Ba'sukkos Hoh'shavty es Bnei Yisroel B'hot'tzi'i Osom Mai'Eretz*

Mitzrayim (I made the children of Israel dwell in booths, when I brought them out of the land of Egypt, Lev. 23:43)—it is incumbent upon us to be aware of it at the time we recite the *bracha* and perform the mitzvah of sukkah. Thus, if the *s'chach* is more than twenty *ammos* high, that awareness might be lacking and the mitzvah would remain unfulfilled. Similarly, Rav Soloveitchik states, because the rabbis of the Talmud go out of their way to inform us in great detail of the events leading up to *nes Hanukkah*, it is incumbent upon us to be aware and to verbalize that awareness at the time we recite *L'Hadlik Ner Shel Hanukkah* by adding the reason for lighting—namely, *She'asa Nissim La'a'vohseinu*. This second *bracha*, which is a *birchas shevach*, indeed explains the reason for our lighting; thus it is not an interruption between the *bracha* and mitzvah, but rather an integral part of the mitzvah itself.

12

Does *Mishenichnas Adar* Apply to *Adar Rishon?*

The *Mishna* (*Megillah* 6b) states that if the *Megillah* (*Megillas Esther*) was read in the first Adar (Adar 1) and *Bais Din* subsequently had prolonged the year by the inclusion of a second Adar, the *Megillah* must be read again in the second Adar. The *Gemorah* quotes a *Tossefta* that discusses a dispute between *Tannoim* on this subject. According to Rabbi Elazar ben Yossi, we need *not* read the *Megillah* in the second Adar. According to Rabbi Shimon ben Gamliel, who agrees with our *Mishna*, we *must* read it again in the second Adar.

The *Gemorah* analyzes each *Tanna*'s reasoning and explains that Rabbi Elazar ben Yossi's opinion is based on *Ain Ma'avirin Al Ha'Mitzvos* (We do not postpone the performance of *Mitzvos*). Once we have the opportunity to read the *Megillah*, we must do so at the earliest moment. In this case, it is the first Adar. The reasoning of Rabbi Shimon ben Gamliel is based on the theory of *M'samech G'ulah Li'G'ulah* (We adjoin one redemption with another redemption—Purim and Pesach). Because the second Adar is closest to *Nissan*, we postpone the observance of Purim to the second Adar.

Many *acharonim*, including the *S'fas Emes*, are puzzled by the reasoning attributed to Rabbi Elazar ben Yossi. *Ain Ma'avarin Al Ha'Mitzvos* only applies when there is a definite mitzvah at hand. Here, however, it is *questionable* whether the first Adar is in fact the right month for the mitzvah. How can we be in violation of *Ain Ma'avirin*?

According to Rav Soloveitchik, the key to understanding the *Gemorah*'s logic is to understand the *uniqueness of the month of Adar*. No other month in which we observe holidays has the distinction of being a "special month." *Mi'Sheh'Nichnas Adar Marbin B'Simcha* ("When Adar begins we enhance our joy) because during this month, the tide turned from sorrow to gladness (*miyogon l'simcha*) for our people. This aspect applies to the entire month of Adar, even the first one." As a matter of fact, according to the Talmud *Yerushalmi*, if a person is unable to read the *Megillah* within the designated days—the eleventh, twelfth, thirteenth, fourteenth, or fifteenth—he may read it any day during the *entire month of* Adar. The *Mechaber* in *Shulchan Oruch* notes this opinion (688:7). Thus, the Rav explains, according to Rabbi Elazar ben Yossi, if we are in such a special month of *simcha* and we do not express our joy by reading the *Megillah*, we are indeed in violation of *Ain Ma'avirin.*

The Halakha follows that of Rabbi Shimon ben Gamliel: we defer the mitzvah of reading the *Megillah* until the second Adar, in compliance with the concept of adjoining the redemption of Purim to that of Pesach. However, the emotional feeling of *marbin b'simcha*, and posting signs to that effect, indeed would be appropriate, for it applies even to the first Adar.

13

Melacha on Purim Night

Rav Josef Caro (*Orach Chaim* 696:1) states that in places where the custom of not engaging in *melacha* on Purim is observed, it is forbidden to work. The *Ramo* adds that our custom today is to observe this prohibition. The *Biur Halakha* notes that the *Pri M'Gadim* limited this restriction only to the day of Purim and not to the night, while the *Chasam Sofer* included even the night.

Rav Soloveitchik felt that the *issur melacha* is not applicable at night. The *Gemorah* (*Megillah* 5b) relates that Rabbi Yehuda Hanasi did *melacha* on Purim: he planted. The *Gemorah* questions how he was permitted to do so and offers two explanations: 1) it was not his *minhag* to abstain from *melacha* on Purim, and 2) his planting was *binyan shel simcha* —a joyous occasion, or planting for joyous purposes.

It was obvious to Rav Soloveitchik that the *issur melacha* discussed was not the same as "resting" on Shabbos or *Yom Tov*, for on Shabbos and *Yom Tov*, *melacha* of *simcha* is never permitted. The type of *melacha* that we are discussing is that which detracts (*hesech hadaas*) from *Simchas* Purim, similar to "working" on *Chol Hamoed* or "work" forbidden to a mourner (*avel*). Because the mitzvah of *simcha* on Purim is limited to the day—*Y'mai Mishteh V'Simcha*—and "work" is not intrinsically forbidden but only abstained from as a detraction of *simcha*, it is a logical conclusion that just as *simcha* does not apply at night, neither does the *hesech hadaas* of *issur melacha*. Therefore, there are no restrictions on working on Purim night.

14

Mechiras Chometz via Telephone or Mail

Our *minhag* is that when we designate a rabbi as a *sheliach* (agent) to sell our *Hometz* to a non-Jew, the rabbi asks us to be *m'kabbel kinyan* to accomplish this designation.

The *Rambam* writes (*Mechira* 5:12 and 5:11 and 5:13) that naming a *sheliach* does not require a *kinyan*: *Yesh D'vorim Harbeh She'ain Tzorich Kinyan, K'gohn . . . Ha'oseh Sheliach* (There are many instances where *kinyan* is not required, such as the designation of an agent). However, . . . *She'no'hagu Rove HameKomos L'haknos L'miktzas D'vorim Eilu* (Many places indeed have a *minhag* to require *kinyan* for some of these instances). He says that although a *kinyan* is not necessary, because the *min-*

hag has been established it should be continued. The *Rambam* concludes that the purpose of this *minhag* was to ensure that the utilization of a *sheliach* should not be taken lightly: *"L'hodiah She'aino Omer D'vorim Eilu K'mischak* (To tell us that his words [regarding *kinyan*] should not be said frivolously)."

Rav Soloveitchik interprets this ruling to mean that a *minhag Yisroel* must be preserved—if not in deed, then at least in spirit. If one is unable to be physically present for *kabbolas kinyan* and makes the arrangement by telephone, he should clearly express to the rabbi that "I am doing this earnestly, with my full heart." If he makes the arrangement by mail, he should sign a formal contract, which would be equivalent to expressing one's earnestness on the telephone. Rav Soloveitchik also suggests that the rabbi request that any individual with the caller give his handkerchief to the caller and act on behalf of the rabbi. This suggestion is based on *Tosfos* (*Kiddushin 26b, Hochi Garsinon*).

15

Using Grape Juice for the Four Cups of Wine at the Seder

Regarding the mitzvah of drinking four cups of wine at the Seder, the *Gemorah* (*Pesachim* 108:b) states: *Shos'son Chai Lo Yotzo L'Gamrei Y'dai Chovoson* (If one drank the wine in a raw state without diluting it with the appropriate proportions of water, he has not fulfilled his mitzvah).

The *Rambam* adds: *Daled Kosos Ha'ailu Tzarich Limzog O'som K'dai Shetihiyoh Shtiyo Areiva, Hakol L'fi Ha'yayin Ul'fi Daas Ha'shoseh* (The four cups must be diluted sufficiently to make the drinking pleasant and pleasing to the drinker, the proportions depending upon the wine at hand and the individual drinker) (*Chometz U'Mata* 7:9).

Accordingly, it is Rav Soloveitchik's opinion that for one who does not enjoy the pleasures of wine but would rather drink grape juice, the grape juice is the *mitzvah min ha'muvchar*, the preferred method of fulfilling the mitzvah. He should be encouraged to drink grape juice exclusively for the mitzvah of *shtiyah*.

However, this is true only for the three last cups at the Seder. Because the first cup also serves as the cup for kiddush, we have to take another aspect into consideration. According to the *Rambam* (*Hilchos Shabbos* 29:14), grape juice is unfit for kiddush because we must use only wine fit for libation on the altar (*l'nasech al hamizbeach*).

However, the *Shulchan Aruch* rules (272:8), like *Tosfos* and the *Rosh*, that grape juice is permissible for kiddush and that the *Gemorah* (*Bava Basra* 97a), in requiring wine fit for the *mizbeach*, only meant to exclude wine that was spoiled or had bad odor, not grape juice.

Nevertheless, Rav Soloveitchik conducted himself according to the *Rambam*'s opinion and avoided grape juice for kiddush. Consequently, because he also felt that the first cup at the Seder serves not only as one of the four required cups but also as the cup of kiddush, he insisted on using only regular, non-*mevushal* wine for the first cup.

Part III

Tefilla and *Davening*

1

A *Bracha* in Vain, Even Without Uttering the Name of *Hashem*

The Torah states: *Lo Sisa Es Shem* (Do not use the name of *Hashem*, your God, in vain) (*Sh'mos 20:7*). In this regard, the *Gemorah* (*Brachos 33a*) says "One who recites a *bracha* that is unnecessary violates the *issur* of '*Lo Sisa.*'"

The *Shulchan Oruch* (*Orach Chaim* 206:6) rules that if one recites a *bracha* over food he is holding in his hand and it accidentally falls, he must recite *another bracha*; he also must add *Baruch Shem K'vod Malchuso L'olam Va-ed* because he said the *Shem Shamayim* in vain.

The general rule regarding *brachos* is *Sofek brachos l'hokail* (A doubtful *bracha* requires leniency). Many *acharonim* explain that this rule is based on the Halakha of not using the name of *Hashem* in vain. Thus, the *bracha* in question perhaps should be recited in a language other than "*Lashon Hakodesh*." This practice would eliminate the violation of *Lo Sisa*, for this only applies to the seven names of *Hashem* that cannot be erased, while at the same time fulfilling the requirement of a *bracha* that can be recited in *any* language (e.g., English).

Rav Soloveitchik suggests that another reason for *Sofek brachos L'hokail* is that we cannot add any *brachos* to those the *Anshei K'nesses Hagdola* instituted, not even to praise *Hashem* (*Megillah* 18a). Therefore, a *Chazzan* should *not* sing an unnecessary *bracha* for entertainment purposes, *even if he uses the expression ADOSHEM ELOKAINU*, because this too fulfills the requirements of a *bracha* and would be the same as using English.

2

Tefillas Haderech on Domestic Flights

Tefillas Haderech is discussed in the *Gemorah* (*Brachos* 29b) and codified in the *Shulchan Oruch* (*Orach Chaim* 110:4–7).

According to Rav Soloveitchik, one need *not* recite the *Tefillas Haderech* on domestic flights if one becomes so used to them that there is no feeling of apprehension when traveling. It is precisely this anxiety that necessitates saying *Tefillas Haderech*. Absence of fear obviates the need to say it.

3

Praying for the Ill

In *Parshas B'Ha'a'los'cha*, Moshe Rabbeinu prays for the recovery of his sister Miriam, who was afflicted with *tzoraas*, by using a five-word prayer: "*KAIL NOH REFOH NOH LOH*" (12:13). Based on this event, Rav Soloveitchik learned several Halakhos.

The *Gemorah* (*Brachos* 34a) states that one who prays on behalf of someone need not mention the sick person's name because Moshe did not mention his sister's name. However, the *Mogen Avraham* (119:1) states, in the name of the *Maharil*, that this practice only applies if the ill person is in our presence. Otherwise, a name must be used.

It is customary to use the ill person's first name and the name of his or her mother. However, it is quoted in *Yesodai Yeshurun* that this is not an absolute necessity and that when the mother's name is not known, the father's name will do just as well.

The *Ramo* (*Yorah Deah* 335:4) quotes the *Bais Yosef*, in the name of the *Ramban*, that wishing a *refuah* to the patient is an integral part of the mitzvah of *bikur cholim*. Without this prayer, the mitzvah of *bikur cholim* is not fulfilled.

The formula of the prayer itself must meet certain guidelines:

1. It must have God's name. Therefore, merely saying Have a *refuah sh'laima* is not enough.
2. The prayer must make reference to all Jewish sick, as is stated in *Yoreh Deah* 335:6: *HAMA-KOM YERACHAIM OLECHO B'SOCH CHOLAI YISROEL*. The *Shach* adds (335:4) that by including others in the prayer, there is a better chance of acceptance.

4

Tefillah as Torah *Sheh B'al Peh*

The *Gemorah* (*Bava Kamo* 82a) states that Ezra (and his *Bais Din*) decreed that a *ba'al-keri*—one who has a seminal emission—must immerse in a mikvah before engaging in Torah and *tefillah*. A later *Bais Din* rescinded this decree.

The *Rambam*'s understanding of this *Gemorah*, based on what he states in *Hilchos Tefillah* (4:4), is that Ezra's rule only regarded learning Torah; a subsequent *Bais Din* expanded the decree to *tefillah*. Just as a *ba'al keri* was prohibited from Torah study without first going to the mikvah, so was he prohibited from *tefillah*. The *Kesef Mishneh* cannot find a source for the inclusion of *tefillah*. However, such a decree did in fact exist, and the *Kesef Mishneh* assumes that it was included in Ezra's original *takonoh* (decree). However, most *Rishonim* concur that the later *Bais Din* rescinded the requirement of mikvah to both Torah *and Tefillah* (*Hilchos Tefillah* 4:5). The question remains: why must we assume that Ezra's *takonoh* regarding Torah also included *tefillah*?

According to Rav Soloveitchik, the concepts of *tefillah* and Torah are inseparable. *Tefillah* is indeed a form of Torah *Sheh B'al Peh*. We find in the *Gemorah* (*Shabbos* 115b) that writing *brachos* using the divine name of *Hashem* is tantamount to burning a *Sefer Torah* because on Shabbos these *brachos* could not be rescued in case of fire, for they were not to be written in the first place. Like Torah *Sheh B'al Peh*—"*LO NISNU L'HIKOSAIV*"—*tefillos* and siddurim were not permitted to be written. Therefore, it is quite understandable that during Ezra's era, many did not know how to daven and were unable to memorize the *Shemonah Eseri*. The need for a *Chazoras HaShat'z* became a necessity. It was only after the ban of writing Torah *Sheh B'al Peh* was lifted because of "*AIS LA'A'SOS LA'HASHEM*" that the ban on writing siddurim and *Machzorim* also was subsequently lifted. Rav Soloveitchik suggests that just as Ezra prohibited the *ba'al keri* from all forms of Torah (written and oral), so too did he prohibit the *ba'al keri* from *tefillah* as well.

Parenthetically, Reb Chaim Soloveitchik made a practice of always davening by heart because he felt that *tefillah* is Torah *Sheh B'al Peh* and, as such, should not be read from a text, if at all possible. As a matter of fact, several weeks before the *Yomim No'ra'im*, he would study the *Machzor* by heart so that he would not have to look into a text for *Tefillas Shemonah Esrei*. However, according to *Mishne Brura* (*Orach Chaim* 53:n87), it is always preferable to daven using a siddur.

5

Understanding the Role of the *Sheliach Tzibbur*

The *Gemorah* (*Brachos* 55a) states that one of the things that curtails a man's days in this world is his refusal to go up to the Torah when called for an *aliyah*. However, if a person is asked to be a *sheliach tzibbur*, it is wrong, even arrogant, if he accepts immediately. Rather, he should refuse twice and only accept when asked a third time. This is an indication of humility.

The basic difference between these two situations is that being called to the Torah is an act of performing a mitzvah. As such, one should act with haste upon receiving the opportunity. When the congregation asks one to be the *sheliach tzibbur*, however, it is not merely an honor; it is a request to be their only representative to *Hashem*. When the *sheliach tzibbur* repeats the *Shemonah Esrei* (*Chazoras Hashatz*), he is standing alone and pleading Hashem on behalf of his congregation and for all *Klal Yisroel*. This is indeed an awesome responsibility, which one must accept with extreme modesty. Only after the third request should this calling be accepted.

According to Rav Soloveitchik, *Chazal* learned this from Moshe Rabbeinu at his encounter with Hashem at the *S'neh* (burning bush). In *Parshas Sh'mos* (3:2), Moshe is charged with the responsibility of saving the Jewish people from their oppression. At first, Moshe is reluctant. For this, the *Gemorah* (*Zevachim* 102a), quoted by *Rashi*, says that he was duly punished. In *Parshas Vaeira* (6:12), Moshe again is charged with a mission; once again he hesitates and says that he is not qualified to be a spokesman for his people. Hashem persists, and Moshe acquiesces, accepting his assignment. This time, however, *Rashi* brings up no talmudic or midrashic source regarding punishment. Why was Moshe not punished as before?

Rav Soloveitchik explains that in *Parshas Sh'mos*, Moshe's mission was simply one of saving the Jewish people from further agony and oppression. This constitutes a call to perform a mitzvah of *hatzoloh*. Therefore, procrastination cannot be tolerated. However, in *Parshas Vaeira*, Moshe was given the mantle of leadership, which, by its very nature, requires humbleness. His response was indeed the correct response of a true Jewish leader. Likewise, *Chazal* felt that one particular Torah *aliyah* is regarded as greater in importance than any other: being called for the last eight *Pesukim* of the Torah. The *Gemorah* (*Bava Basra* 15a) states that *Yochid Koreh Ohsom* — a *yochid* should read these last eight *Pesukim*; a *yochid* can refer to someone special whom the congregation reveres. When we read these *Pesukim* on *Simchas* Torah—the only time we read them—we refer to the one honored with this *aliyah* as "*Chosson* Torah." In an effort to meet the requirement of being called three times before accepting this exalted honor, the *gabbai* will recite the *Birshus*, which calls the person three times: *Amod, Amod, Amod.*

6

Tefillas Maariv as *Tefillas Reshus*

Chazal tells us (*Brachos* 26a) that our Avos—Avraham, Yitzchok, and Yaakov—established our Tefillos. Avraham is identified with *"Tefillas Shacharis,"* Yitzchok is credited with *"Tefillas Mincha,"* and Yaakov instituted *"Tefillas Maariv."*

That same *Gemorah*, however, records another opinion: that our *Tefillos* were created to commemorate the daily sacrifices in the *Bais Ha-Mikdosh*. The simple understanding of the *Gemorah* is that both opinions are correct and complement each other. Our *Avos* indeed established the three *tefillos*, but the pattern, frequency, and timing of each follows that of the daily *korbonos*.

The question, however, is where exactly *"Tefillas Maariv"* fits into all this, for there were only *two* daily sacrifices: the *tomid-shel-shacharis* (morning) and the *tomid-shel-bain-Ha'arbayim* (afternoon). This very question prompted a *Tannaic* dispute. According to *Rabban Gamliel*, the obligation to daven *Maariv* remains an obligation (*chova*). Rabbi Yehoshua maintains it is only optional (*r'shus*). The *Gemorah* later (*Brachos* 27b) cites this dispute among *Amoraim*: *Abaye* followed the opinion of *Rabban Gamliel*, and *Rava* followed that of Rabbi Yehoshua, who stated that *Maariv* is a *reshus*.

In the Halakha, the *Rambam* decides (*Hilchos Tefilla* 1:6, 3:6, and 3:7) in favor of *Rava*—that *Maariv* is a *reshus*—and adds that this is why there is no *Chazoras Hashatz* by *Maariv*. The *Rif*, however, adds (*Daf* 19) that it is "optional" only if one has never davened *Maariv* at all; if one has done so, it is as if he has accepted an obligation, and thus it becomes mandatory. Today, we regard *Maariv* as mandatory because we have chosen to accept it. For this reason, if one fails to recite *V'SAIN TAL U'MOTOR* during the winter months *even for Maariv, the Shemonah Esrei must be repeated* (*Orach Chaim* 114:5).

Rav Soloveitchik connected this idea of "obligation" to daven a *"Tefillas Reshus"* with an unusual Halakha in *Rambam* (*Hilchos Tefillah* 10:6). If one is in doubt whether he *davened*, he is permitted to daven again, provided he has in mind that his second *tefillah* is to be regarded as a *nedavah*, a voluntary *tefillah*. However, if someone begins "*Shemonah Esrei*" and then remembers in the middle that he already *davened*, he must stop immediately, even in the middle of a *bracha*. If, however, this happens during *Maariv*, he may continue the *Shemonah Esrei*. The Rav explains that *Shacharis* and *Mincha* are essentially obligatory *tefillos*. Therefore, by beginning a "*Tefillas Chova*," one cannot continue with a "*Tefillas Nedavah*." However, when davening *Maariv*, which is essentially a "*Tefillas Reshus*" and *thus analogous to a "Tefillas Nedavah,"* if he at any point realizes that he already has davened, he may complete that *Shemonah Esrei*.

7

Stepping out of Shul When Not Davening with the *Tzibbur*

The *Mishna* (*Brachos* 20a) states that a *ba'al-keri*, who in those days was prohibited to study Torah, should think the words of *Shma Yisroel* (*Mehar'her*) when the congregation is reciting the *shma*. The reason offered in the *Gemorah* is that it is not proper for the *tzibbur* to be engaged in *Kabbolas Ohl Malchus Shomayim* while he sits idle.

Based on this conclusion, it is our custom that when a person is present while the *tzibbur* is reciting *Krias Shma*, even though he is not davening, he nevertheless recites the first *Posuk* with them and demonstrates his participation by covering his eyes.

This is also the basis of our *minhag* that when the congregation is reciting *yizkor*, those who are *not* participating should step out of the sanctuary.

Rav Soloveitchik therefore suggests that when the *tzibbur* is davening *Shemonah Esrei* and a person is not davening with them, he also should *step out of the sanctuary* so as not to appear out of place by not participating.

8

Not Saying *Mizmor Shir* Before *Baruch Sheomar*

Although davening daily is a biblical obligation upon every Jewish male and female (*Rambam, Hilchos Tefillah* 1:1 and 1:2), *Chazal* also regard it as a distinct privilege. How could we, mortal human beings, have the freedom and audacity to feel that we can approach the Supreme Master of the universe whenever and wherever we wish and expect Him to listen to our requests—or our praises? Even an audience with a low-ranking public official requires an appointment involving red-tape bureaucracy. Yet we have that privilege with the *Ribono Shel Olum*.

What right do we have to assume such a privilege? By virtue of the *Anshei Knesses HaG'dola*, who gave us this *matir* some 2,400 years ago through the *bracha* of "*Baruch Sheomar*," the opening of *P'sukai D'zimrah*. According to tradition, the script of this opening prayer fell from heaven into the hands of this great body of rabbis and prophets. In this prayer we find the words *Uv'shirai Dovid Av'decha Ne'ha'lel'cha* (And through the Psalms of David your servant we shall praise You). Thus, our privilege to praise *Hashem* is only because King David had done so in the past and had given us the proper vernacular to do so in the present.

According to Rav Soloveitchik, based on this analysis, absolutely no praise or *T'hillim* may be recited *before Baruch Sheomar*. It is a common custom to begin with recitation of *Mizmor Shir Chanukas Habayis* before *Baruch Sheomar*, according to *Nussach Ash'k'naz*. Because we end the *korbonos* section with the *Y'hi Rotzon. . . . Sheyiboneh Bais Hamikdosh Bim'haira V'yomainu*, a prayer for rebuilding the *Bais Hamikdosh*, it behooves us to follow with *Mizmor Shir Chanukas Habayis*.

Not so, Rav Soloveitchik felt. It was the *minhag* of the Rav not to say *Mizmor Shir* or any other phrases of *t'hillim* before the *matir* of *Baruch Sheomar*.

9

Covering One's Head During Davening

The *Gemorah* (*Shabbos* 10a) states that the members of the formal *Bais Din* would begin their sessions by attiring themselves with a *tallis* over their heads (*Mi'sheh'yisatfu Ha-Dayyanim*). *Rashi* comments that the reason for requiring *atifa* (head covering) is because of the presence of the *Shekhinah* when the *Bais Din* is in session ("God stands in the Divine assembly," Ps. 82). *Atifah*, therefore, is for *Kavod Ha-Shekhinah*.

Yom Kippur, too, is a time when the divine presence of the *Shekhinah* is in our midst. The Midrash comments that the reason for blowing the shofar and reciting "*Hashem Hu Ho-Elokim*" seven times at the conclusion of *N'illa* is to mark the *Sheninah*'s departure as it ascends to the seventh rung of heaven. Similarly, at the conclusion of the revelation of *Har Sinai*, we are told (Exod. 19:13) that with the extended blast of the *shofar*, it was once again permissible to ascend the mountain because the *Shekhinah* has left our midst (see *Rashi*). Therefore, according to Rav Soloveitchik, throughout all davening on Yom Kippur, it is proper for everyone to wear their *tallis* over their heads. He even recommends this to unmarried men as well, though a formal hat would be an acceptable substitute.

Likewise, the *Mishna Berura* requires *atifa* while standing *Shemonah Esrei* and for *Birkas Ha-Mozon* (*Orach Chaim* 183: 11). Here, too, a formal hat is the accepted norm. Needless to say, where it is customary, the attire should include a jacket and tie.

10

Facing East or Facing the *Aron Hakodesh*

According to Rav Soloveitchik, the question concerning which direction to face when davening is based on a *tosefta* (*Megillah* 3:14). The *Shulchan Oruch* (*Orach Chaim* 150:5) concludes from this *tosefta* that the entrance to a shul should be opposite the *aron hakodesh* so that, upon entering the shul, one can bow to the *aron hakodesh*, which faces *Eretz Yisroel*—eastward. This direction is also the one in which we stand *Shemonah Esrei*.

In the event that the *aron hakodesh* is not facing *mizrach*, which direction do we face when davening *Shemonah Esrei*: East or the *aron hakodesh*?

Rav Soloveitchik notes that this point is a dispute between *Rashi* and *Tosfos* (*Brachos* 6b). According to

Rashi, if one is davening outside the shul, adjacent to the *aron hakodesh*, he should face the *aron hakodesh*, even though he in essence will be facing west while all the *mispallelim inside* the shul will be facing east. According to *Tosfos*, he should position himself in the same direction as the *mispallelim*, facing east even though he will have his back to the *aron hakodesh*. *Rashi* believed the *aron hakodesh* dominates, while *Tosfos* believed the *mizrach* direction prevails.

Rav Soloveitchik felt that in this situation, we should adopt the rules of *Tosfos* and face *Eretz Yisroel*. However, we must follow the *tzibbur*. If everyone is facing the *aron hakodesh*, it is prohibited for an individual to face elsewhere (*D'mech'zeh K'shtai R'shuyos*) (It appears as two deities). The *Biur* Halakha arrives at a similar conclusion, though from a different perspective.

11

Hoicheh Kedusha: Reciting Shemonah Esrei Simultaneously with the Sheliach Tzibbur

In a situation where a *Hoicheh kedusha* is necessary, such as in cases of *she'as hadechak*, the question always arises: should the individual wait and listen to the *Sheliach Tzibbur* recite the beginning of *"Shemonah Esrei"* until *kedusha* and then begin his own recitation after *"Hakel Hakodosh"* is said, or should the individual immediately begin his *Shemonah Esrei* and say it simultaneously with the *Sheliach Tzibbur?*

This point is a difference of opinion between the *Ramo* and the *Mishne Berurah*, as discussed in the *Biur* Halakha. The *Ramo* states in *Orach Chaim* 124:2:

Vehatzibbur Mispallelim Imo Mila B'Mila Ad Le'acher Ha'Kail Hakodos (The congregation davens with him word for word, until after *Ha'kail Hakodosh*). However, the *Biur* Halakha states: *D'B'Rov Nohagim Hatzibbur L'hamtin Ad She'ye'sahyem Ha'Shatz Ha'Kail Hakodosh* (The congregation waits until after the *Sheliach Tzibbur* finishes *Ha'kail Hakodosh*).

Rav Soloveitchik agreed with the *Ramo*. *Kedusha*, he states, cannot be recited as an isolated praise but must be included in the framework of *Shemonah Esrei*. Under normal circumstances, when the *Sheliach Tzibbur* repeats the *Shemonah Esrei*, he is repeating it not merely for himself but for each individual listening to *Tefillas Ha'Tzibbur*; as such, each individual is regarded as being *B'tohch Ha'T'filla*. However, during a *Hoicheh kedusha*, there is no *Chazoras Ha'Shatz*, and when the *shatz* speaks the *Shemonah Esrei* aloud, he is saying it *only for himself*. For the individual to be considered *B'tohch Ha'tfilla*, he *must* say the *Shemonah Esrei Mila B'mila* with the *shatz*. Only then will his *kedusha* be regarded as within the framework of *Shemonah Esrei*.

Furthermore, according to *Minhag Ashk'naz*, he should not say the usual *Atoh Koddosh*, but rather *Ledor Vador* together with the *shatz*, because that verse is part of the *kedusha* usually recited only by the *Sheliach Tzibbur* and which the individual in this instance, is integrating with his own *Shemonah Esrei*.

12

Responding to *Kedusha* During Silent *Shemonah Esrei*

It is not unusual to find ourselves in the middle of our silent *Shemonah Esrei* while the congregation is already reciting the *kedusha* from *Chazoras HaShatz*. How does one conduct himself in this situation?

Rashi (*Sukka* 38b) raises this very question, and his solution is to stop, davening momentarily, listen attentively to the *kedusha* of the *Sheliach Tzibbur*, and have in mind to fulfill the requirement of *kedusha* using the rule of *Shomai-Ah K'oneh*. Afterward, one continues with silent *Shemonah Esrei*. The novelty of this approach, which happens to be the one most people accept, is that one can fulfill the obligation of reciting *kedusha* without it *not being considered an interruption* (*hefsek*) in the *Shemonah Esrei*.

Tosfos disagrees, arguing that if *Shomai-Ah K'oneh* works so effectively and it is as if one had recited *kedusha*, then by definition it must be regarded as a *hefsek* in *Shemonah Esrei*. Therefore, *Tosfos* concludes, *no silent pause is allowed.*

A third opinion is found in the *Ritvah*, who states that *Shomai-Ah K'oneh* works *only* if a person really is able to say it himself but would rather listen to someone else. However, if he is unable to say it himself, like the situation of *kedusha* in the middle of *Shemonah Esrei*, then *Shomai-Ah K'oneh* will not work. (*Kol Ha-ro'uy L'hila Ain Hila M'akeves Bo*). Thus, he suggests that a person continue his own *tefillah* and ignore the *kedusha*.

Rav Soloveitchik also felt that one cannot be *yotzei* the *kedusha* of *Chazoras HaShatz* just by listening silently. His reasoning is different, however, from that of *Tosfos* or *Ritvah*. Based on the *Rambam*, Rav Soloveitchik felt that for *Tefillas HaTzibbur*, which is *Chazoras HaShatz* and *kedusha*, a verbal response of the *tzibbur* is essential, such as saying amen or the responsive phrases of *kedusha*. *Shomai-ah K'oneh* by itself is not sufficient.

Rav Soloveitchik drew his opinion from his keen inference of the *Rambam*'s statement in *Brachos* 1:11 that a *bracha* can be fulfilled through *Shomei-Ah K'oneh even without responding* amen. However, saying amen becomes tantamount to verbalizing the *bracha* itself. Based on this thought, the Rav believed that in order to be included in *Tefillas HaTzibbur*, every person is required actively to verbalize the "amen" or the responsive phrases of *kedusha*. In our situation, however, one cannot verbalize the *kedusha* response. Therefore, the Rav felt it is best to continue davening without pausing.

13

The *Sheliach Tzibbur* and *Modim D'Rabbonon*

It is a biblical requirement to express gratitude—*ho'daah* (thanks)—to a benefactor. Leah expresses *ho'daah* to *Hashem* upon the birth of her fourth son, stating: *Ha-Paam Odeh Es Hashem, Al Kain Kor'oh Es Sh'mo Yehuda* (This time I must thank *Hashem*, and she called his name *Yehuda*) (*Braishis* 29:35).

Chazal, in formulating the basic *tefillah* of *Shemonah Esrei* saw fit to conclude the third section with *Modim Anachnu Loch—Ho'daah*. When the *Sheliach Tzibbur* repeats the *Shemonah Esrei*, the *tzibbur* listens attentively and answers amen after each *bracha*. However, when the *Sheliach Tzibbur* recites *Modim*, the *tzibbur* recites the *Modim D'Rabbonon* simultaneously (*Sota* 40a).

Why is it that for the entire *Shemonah Esrei* we merely listen attentively but by *modim* we have to express ourselves to *Hashem*? The *Avudraham* states that one can designate another person as an agent (*sheliach*) to perform the task for any request of praise, but when it comes to saying thank you, the beneficiary himself must verbalize it. Thus, *Modim D'Rabbonon* was instituted. But a serious question remains: how can we say *Modim D'Rabbonon* while we listen attentively to the *Sheliach Tzibbur* saying the regular *modim*?

A similar question arises in the *Gemorah* (*Sota* 40a) concerning the *p'sukim* that the congregation recites while the *kohanim* are blessing them with *Birkas Kohanim*. How can we listen attentively to these *brachos* while simultaneously reciting *p'sukim*? The *Tur* therefore writes (*Orach Chaim* 128) that it is better *not to recite the p'sukim*, but rather to listen and concentrate on the *Birkas Kohanim*.

According to Rav Soloveitchik, because the *Modim D'Rabbonon* is a basic requirement, it should be recited in the following way: the *Sheliach Tzibbur* begins saying *modim* out loud, then pauses long enough for the *tzibbur* to say the *Modim D'Rabbonon*. He then completes the rest of *modim* out loud. In this manner we can satisfy our need to express our thanks yet listen to every word of *Chazoras Ha-Shatz*.

14

A Nonobservant
Koben Duchening

The *Shulchan Aruch* (*Orach Chaim* 128:37), based
on the *Gemorah* (*M'nochos* 59a), states that a *Kohen*
who worships idols is prohibited from *Duchening*.
According to many authorities—*Rambam*, *Rashi*,
Rabbeinu Gershon—even if he subsequently does
teshuva (repentance), the prohibition remains. The
Mishna Berura (note134) adds that this ban also applies to a *M'chalel* Shabbos (a non-*shomer* Shabbos).

The source of this stringency is the *Rambam*,
who clearly states (*Hilchos Bi'as Mikdash* 9:13) that
a *Kohen* idol worshiper, whether he worships inten-
tionally or unintentionally, may never serve in the
Mikdash (Holy Temple), even if he does *teshuva*.

Rav Soloveitchik interpreted the *Rambam* to mean that regarding service in the *Mikdash*, we have a unique Halakha that disqualifies an idol worshiper even after he does *teshuva*. It has nothing to do with the individual person (*gavra*), for once a Jew does *teshuva* sincerely, he is totally forgiven for his transgression. However, regarding the *Mikdash*, it is a special Halakha of *Mo-us Li-G'voha* (abomination to God).

Consequently, the Rav disagreed with the *Mishna Berura*, as did his father, Rabbi Moshe Soloveitchik, and said that the stringency of an idol worshiper should not be extended to a Shabbos violator. On the contrary, if such a *Kohen* does indeed come to shul and wants to *duchen*, we should not reject him but encourage him to do this mitzvah of *duchening*. Perhaps it will lead him to do other mitzvos and eventually do *teshuva Gemurah*.

Rav Moshe Feinstein, zt"l, came to the same conclusion as the Rav, but from a different perspective (*Iggros Moshe, Orach Chaim* 1:33).

15

Saying the *Kedusha* of *Uvaletzion* Without a Minyan

The *Ramo* (*Orach Chaim* 25:3) states that there are three *kedushos* we recite every weekday morning: *kedusho* of *Yotzer Ohr*, *Chazoras Ha-Shatz*, and *Uvaletzion*. The *Mishna Berura* (note 55) and *Behr Haitev* (note 3) quote many *Acharonim* who say that we have four *kedushos*, including the *Borchu* as the fourth *kedusha*.

Whether there are three or four *kedushos*, all agree that *Uvaletzion* is in fact a recognized *kedusha*. Indeed, the *Gemorah* refers to it as "*Kedusha D'sidrah*" (*Sota* 49a). This prompted *Chazal* to question whether in fact an individual may recite "*Uvaletzion*" without a minyan because a *Dovor Sh'Bik'Dusha* requires an absolute minyan. The *Ramo* (*Orach Chaim* 132:1), however, declares that the predominant custom is to allow its recitation even *without a minyan*. We regard the *kedusha* of "*Uvaletzion*" as similar to that of *kedusha Yotzer Ohr*, which, according to all authorities, can be recited without standing and without a minyan.

According to Rav Soloveitchik, when the *Sheliach Tzibbur* reads the three verses of *Uvaletzion* aloud, as is the custom in many communities, and the congregation responds with *Kodosh-Kodosh-Kodosh*, *Boruch K'vod*, and *Hashem Yimloch*, this is a clear indication that *Uvaletzion* is intended as a real *kedusha* and *cannot be recited in the absence of a minyan*. If there is no minyan, the Rav did not permit the *Sheliach Tzibbur* to recite the three verses aloud.

16

Not To Remove the *Tefillin* Until After *Aleinu*

According to many sources, including Rav Hai Gaon, *Y'hoshua* composed the text of *Aleinu* after he led *B'nai Yisroel* across the Jordan River. During the talmudic period, it was part of the Rosh Hashana *Mussof Shemonah Esrei*. Some time later, it was incorporated into the daily davening as a conclusion to *tefillah*.

The *Shulchon Oruch* (*Orach Chaim* 25:13) states that it is customary not to remove one's *tefillin* until after the *kedusha* of *Uvaletzion*. At this point, *tefillah* is officially over. However, the *Ramo* adds, according to *Kabbala*, it is proper not to remove the *tefillin* until after the *three kedushos and four kaddishim*. Most *Acharonim* disagree with the *Ramo*, as noted in *Mishneh Berura* (note 55), for they cannot find the source for four kaddishim. The three kaddishim are after *Yishtabach, Chazoras Ha-Shatz,* and *Uvaletzion* (excluding all of the mourners' kaddishim, for we are only referring to the kaddish of the *Sheliach Tzibbur*). Where is the *Ramo*'s fourth kaddish? The *Acharonim* conclude that the *Ramo* must have erred and instead of three *kedushos* and four kaddishim, he really meant four *kedushos* and three kaddishim. The *Acharonim* regard "*Borchu*" as the first *kedusha*; the sitting *kedusha* of *B'Sofo B'Rura U'vin'Ima* within the *bracha* of *Yotzer Ohr* as the second; the standing *kedusha* of *Chazoras Ha-Shatz* as the third; and the *kedusha* of *Uvaletzion* as the fourth, which concludes the *tefillah*.

According to Rav Soloveitchik, the *Ramo* as written is not in error. The *Ramo* felt that the kaddish following *Aleinu* is not merely a mourner's kaddish" but rather a *Sheliach Tzibbur's* kaddish that can be delegated to a mourner or any other person. The *Ramo* states so specifically in 132:2 that in the event there is no mourner present, any other person should recite this kaddish, even if he is not a mourner and *even if his parents are alive. He may recite the kaddish after Aleinu, for it is an integral part of tefillah*. Thus, the Rav states, the *Ramo* was precise and correct when he stated that *tefillin* should not be removed until after the fourth kaddish, which is in fact the end of *tefillah* and not the *Uvaletzion*, as the *Mechaber* states.

Part IV
"Krias HaTorah"

1

"Krias HaTorah"
Without a *Kohen*

It is a common practice in many congregations that when a need arises for two yisraelim to receive an *aliyah* to the Torah on Monday, Thursday, or Shabbos afternoon, we ask the *kohanim* present either to "forgive" their due honor in favor of the yisraelim or to step out of the shul so that in their absence a *Yisrael* can be called in their place.

This practice of circumventing the *"Kedushas Kohen"* is not suggested in *Shulchan Aruch* and certainly not recommended. As a matter of fact, the *Ramo* emphatically states (*Orach Chaim* 135:1) that it is preferable to *add a fourth aliyah* under certain circumstances rather than circumvent the mitzvah of *"V'Kidahsto"* of the *kohen*. True, the *Mishna Berura* adds that we don't follow the practice of the *Ramo* today; however, the *Chofetz Chaim* does not suggest an alternative solution.

According to Rav Soloveitchik, our common practice is absolutely not in conformance with Halakha and therefore not advisable. The *Gemorah* (*Megillah* 21b) asks: "To what do the three *aliyos* correspond?" Rav Assi answers: "To Torah, *N'vi'im*, and *K'suvim*." This means that the Torah itself incorporates within itself all three *kedushos*: "*Kedushas* Torah," *Kedushas N'vi'im*, and *Kedushas K'suvim*. *Rovo* answers that the three *aliyos* correspond to "*Kohen, Levi*, and *Yisrael*."

We see from the above that the reason for calling a *kohen* first to the Torah is not only because of *V'Kidashto*, as the *Gemorah Gittin* suggests, but also because it is an integral part of the mitzvah of *Krias HaTorah*. Therefore, according to Rav Soloveitchik, if there is no *kohen* for the first *aliyah* for any reason, the completeness of *Kiyyum Krias HaTorah Bishlaimus* is lacking.

2

Benching Gomel at *Krias HaTorah*

The *Gemorah* (*Brachos* 54b) states that there are four individuals whose circumstances mandate the offering of thanksgiving: one who has crossed the sea (*Arbo'oh Tzrichin L'hodos*), one who has traversed the wilderness, one who has recovered from an illness, and a prisoner who has been set free. There is a dispute in *Gemorah* (*M'Nochos* 79b) between *Rashi* and *Tosfos* whether this means that the individual concerned is required to bring a *korban* (sacrifice) *todah* or if he merely is required to recite the *bracha* of *HaGomel*.

In the absence of a *Bais HaMikdash*, the *korban todah* is not a feasible option. But the *Birchas Ha-Gomel* is very much in the realm of Halakha. The

103

Mechaber in *Shulchan Oruch* (*Orach Chaim* 219:3) quotes the *Gemorah* in *Brachos* that *"Birchas Ha-Gomel"* must be said in the presence of a minyan (at least ten adult males). He also quotes *Tosfos* in *Brachos* that the prevailing custom is to recite this *bracha* only during *Krias HaTorah*. His reasoning is that during *Krias HaTorah*, you always are guaranteed that a minyan is present.

According to Rav Soloveitchik, there is a further dimension to the requirement that the *"Birchas Ha-Gomel"* be recited in conjunction with the Torah reading. When the Torah is lying on the *bimah* (*shulchan*), the combination of the two constitutes a simulation of the *mizbai'ach*, which is where the *korban todah* would have been offered. Thus, by requiring the recitation of the *bracha* during *Krias HaTorah*, we are fulfilling both aspects: the verbalization of *Birchas HaGomel and the simulation of a korban todah upon the mizbai'ach*. This satisfies the opinions of *Rashi* and *Tosfos*.

3

Reading *Yissachar* With a Double Letter *Sinn*

Although the name Yissachar is always written as
Yissasschar with a double letter *sinn*, the way we
read it depends upon a variety of *minhagim*. Some
regard it as an ordinary *K'Siv* and *K'Ri* situation, in
which case it is always read as *Yissachar* with one
"*sinn*." Many communities follow the custom of reading it with a double the first time it appears (Gen.
30:18) and thereafter with only a single.

Rav Soloveitchik insisted that in his presence the
Baal Koreh read the name with a double *sinn* every
time it appears in the Torah—until the reading of
Parshas Pinchas, when the pronunciation reverts
back to one *sinn*. The Rav based his decision on a
midrash, quoted by the *Da'as Z'kainim*, that after

Yissachar married and had four sons, he named one of them Yov (Gen. 46:13). He subsequently realized that Yov was also the name of an idol, and because a name, once given, cannot simply be revoked, he chose to change it by taking one *sinn* from his own name and adding it to his son's. Thus, he became Yissachar and his son became Yoshuv (*Bamidbar* 26:24).

Rav Soloveitchik was as fastidious with pronunciation of biblical names during *Krias HaTorah* as he was with other words that the *Baal Koreh* meticulously had to verbalize.

4

The Torah Reading on *Simchas* Torah

The *Gemorah* (*Megillah* 31a) states that on the last day of Sukkos, we read from *Kol Ha-B'Chor* (*D'VORIM* 15:19) and on the next day (referring to *Yom Tov Sheni* in the Diaspora, known to us as *Simchas* Torah) we read "*V'Zos Ha-B'Rocho.*" The *HafTorah* is *Vaya'-Amod Shlomo* (*Melachim* 1:8).

We know that every *Yom Tov* Torah reading must relate directly to the theme of that respective *Yom Tov*, as was ordained by *Moshe Rabbeinu*, for the *Gemorah Megillah* says: *Va-Y'Daber Moshe Es Mo-Adei Hashem El B'Nai Yisroel, Sh'Yihiyu Korin Kol Echod Bi-Z'Mano* (31a). What is the thematic relation between *Simchas* Torah and *V'Zos Ha-B'Rocho*? When we read the Torah on an ordinary Shabbos, there need not be a relationship between the weekly *parsha* and the calendar week it is being read. But on *Yom Tov* the Halakha demands that the existing relationship be discernable as a *mattir* for it to be read. So what is the connection here?

According to Rav Soloveitchik, the connection is found in the *Gemorah* (*Sukkah* 48a), which states that *Shemini Atzeres* is an independent *Yom Tov*, separate from the rest of Sukkos, in six aspects, as noted by the acrostic P-Z-R-K-S-H-B. The "B" stands for *bracha*, or blessing. *Rashi* explains, based on the *Tosefta*, that on the eighth day of Sukkos, the people blessed the king (1 Kings 8:66). However, it also states in that same chapter that the king blessed the nation (8:55). It was a reciprocal blessing: the people to their king, and the king to his nation. *Moshe Rabbeinu* was regarded as a king, for it says: *Va-Y'Hi Bi'Y'Shurun Melech* (He became king over *Yeshurun*) (*D'vorim* 33:5); as king at the end of his life, he blessed the people of Israel in *V'Zos Ha-B'Rocho*. Therefore, in *Chutz La'Aretz* on *Simchas* Torah, we read this selection, which is considered the second half of *Shemini Atzeres*, as a fulfillment of the "B" *bracha* aspect of this *Yom Tov*.

5

Priorities in Torah Reading on Shabbos Hanukkah and Rosh Chodesh

Tosfos (*Shabbos* 23b) says, in the name of the *Rashba*, that because we have two special *HafToros* to read—namely, that of Rosh Chodesh and of Hanukkah—we select that of Hanukkah because of *Pirsumei Nisa*. The rule of *Tadir V'sh'aino Tadir* (What occurs more often, versus what occurs less often), would not apply, for it only applies when there is a question of priority—which comes first and which comes second. The rule is not operative when only one *HafTorah* is read.

Once the *HafTorah* has been selected, the Torah reading automatically falls into place because the *HafTorah* must relate to the final Torah segment. Of the three Torah scrolls that are taken out, the third must be used for Hanukkah, and the second for Rosh Chodesh. In addition, the rule of *tadir* dictates here that Rosh Chodesh come first and Hanukkah last because we are going to read from two scrolls.

The *Mechaber* (*Orach Chaim* 684:3 note 9) codifies this procedure and adds that we have six *aliyos* from the *parsha* of the week in the first *Sefer*; the seventh *aliyah* is that of Rosh Chodesh (from the second *Sefer*), and the *maftir* for Hanukkah is read from the third *Sefer*. The *Mishna Berura* (9) adds that the six *aliyos* from the first *Sefer* are not meant as a limitation, but only as a minimum, for we can add as many *hosofos* as we desire.

According to Rav Soloveitchik, this interpretation is not correct. He had a tradition, passed down from his father and grandfather, that the Rosh Chodesh Torah reading must be one of the basic seven *aliyos* or a *maftir*. It never can be read as a mere *hosofa*. Consequently, we cannot make *hosofos* in the first *Sefer* so that the Rosh Chodesh reading indeed will be one of the basic seven *aliyos*.

6

Standing During the *Aseres Hadibros*

The *Rambam* was asked whether it's proper or even required to stand during the reading of the *Aseres Hadibros*. His response was clear and emphatic (*Teshuvos Ha'Rambam* 60): based upon the *Gemorah* (*Brachos* 12a), it is absolutely *prohibited* to stand because to do so would give credence to those who believe that the Ten Commandments are more important than the rest of the mitzvos.

What makes this situation so puzzling is that it has become a universal custom to do what the *Rambam* clearly prohibits. We stand during the reading of *Aseres Hadibros* on all three occasions— *Parshiyos Yisro*, *Vo'Eschanan*, and *Shavuos*. How has a *minhag* that ignores the *Rambam*'s sharp admonition evolved?

For Rav Soloveitchik, the answer lies in that we have two distinct ways of reading the *Aseres Hadibros*: *taam tachton* (reading according to the bottom notations of the words) and *taam elyon* (reading according to the notations on top of the words). With *taam tachton*, we read the words based on verses (*p'sukim* of Torah), while with *taam elyon* we read the words based on separating the commandments (*dibros*). For example, according to *elyon*, all the verses pertaining to the commandment of Shabbos are read as if they are one verse because they are indeed one *dibur* (mitzvah); however, the commandments of *Lo-Tirtzoch*, *Lo-Tinof*, *Lo-Tignov*, and *Lo-Sa'Aneh* are read as four separate verses because they are indeed four separate *dibros*.

Torah reading per se is fulfilled by reading written *p'sukim* according to *taam tachton* and is thus a *kiyyum* of Talmud Torah. Many communities customarily read the *Aseres Hadibros* according to *taam tachton* on Shabbos *Parshas Yisro* and Shabbos *Parshas Vo'Eschanon*. However, on *Shavuos*, there is another perspective for the Torah reading, namely that of commemorating *Ma'amod Har-Sinai*, which is symbolized by reading according to *taam elyon*. The *Rambam* did not object to standing for the sake of the commemoration.

Since the issue of the *Rambam*'s *teshuva*, the prevailing custom has been to read the Torah with *taam elyon*, even on Shabbos *Yisro* and Shabbos *Vo'Eschanon*, in addition to *Yom Tov Shavuos*. Consequently, because we stand during the reading of *Aseres Hadibros* as a *zecher* to *Ma'Amod Har-Sinai*, it is not negating the *Rambam*'s ruling.

V

Questions Pertaining to *Aveilus*

1

Nichum Aveilim as Part of *Nihug Aveilus*

The *Gemorah* (*Shabbos* 152a) states that if a person dies without any *aveilim* to mourn him, then ten men are requested to sit shiva in his residence and the rest of the community is to be "*menachem.*" The *Rambam* codifies this practice in *Aveil 13:4*.

According to Rav Soloveitchik, *nichum aveilim* is an integral part of *nihug aveilus* for the mourner. It is a *kiyyum* of his fulfillment of *aveilus*, and the *aveil* has to perform a concrete act, such as nodding his head, to acknowledge the *nichum*.

On the morning of the seventh day, before the *aveil* gets up from shiva, he must fulfill his *kiyyum* of *aveilus* by waiting until someone is *menachem* him (*Moed Koton* 19b).

An *aveil* is not exempt from the mitzvah to be *menachem* others. Therefore, if more than one *aveil* are sitting together, each has a *chiyyuv* of being *menachem* the others.

When two or more *aveilim* are sitting together, it is proper for visitors to be *menachem* each one separately, rather than all of them together.

2

Bringing a *Sefer* Torah to the Home of an *Aveil*

The *mechayev* (need) to take out two *Sifrei* Torah on certain Shabbosos is because the readings are in two different places. Even if they were just a few *amudim* apart, it nevertheless would take a few moments to be *gollel* from one *amud* to the other. However, had there been no need to be *gollel*, it would not be permitted to take out two *Sifrei* Torah. Hypothetically, on *Parshas Shekalim*, had the regular *Parsha* been *Tetzaveh* (In reality this cannot happen because nowadays *Shekalim* cannot fall on *Tetzaveh* or *Ki Sissa—Kesef Mishna* on *Hilchos Tefillah* 13:22), we would not be permitted to take out two *Sifrei* Torah. Announcing *Shekalim* is not a sufficient *mechayev* for taking out an additional *Sefer*; there has to be a justifiable need for avoiding *gollel* (*Rambam Tefillah* 13:22).

According to Rav Soloveitchik, even removing one *Sefer* requires a specific *mechayev*: a *tzibbur* requiring a Torah reading. Thus, the *Mechaber* is reluctant to allow bringing a *Sefer* Torah into an *aveil*'s house. Our *minhag* of permitting it is based on the *Ramo* (*Yoreh Deah* 393:3). The minhag that requires reading from it at least three times (*Aruch Hashulchon* 135:32) is a mere *chumra* and not *M'ikar HaDin*. This *chumra* only applies when the *Sefer* Torah has to remain on a table, which is not the proper *kavod HaTorah*. But if it is kept in a small *Aron Hakodesh*, then there are no restrictions necessary. However, Rav Moshe Feinstein, *zt"l*, (*LeTorah V'Hora'ah*, vol. 10) recommends reading it three times under all circumstances.

3

Covering Mirrors in the Home of an *Aveil*

It has been a long-standing tradition to cover the mirrors in the home of someone sitting shiva, from the moment of death to the end of shiva. However, this custom's origin is uncertain, as it does not appear in the *Mishna* or *Gemorah*.

Rav Soloveitchik felt that every *minhag* has its origin in Halakha and that the practice of covering mirrors stems from the concept of *aveilus* in the Talmud.

The *Gemorah* (*Moed Katan* 15a) finds biblical sources for every activity forbidden to mourners, except that of "overturning the beds," known as *K'Fias Ha-Mita*, which the *Gemorah* ascribes to a theory rather than a specific verse. *Bar Kappora* taught (*Moed Katan* 15b) that because man was created in the image of God, he derives from that resemblance his dignity and value. With the death of one of God's creatures, the very image of the Creator Himself is diminished. The overturned bed symbolizes this idea by reminding us that intimate marital relations are to be suspended during this period.

The *Baalei HaTosfos* (*Moed Katan* 21a) offer two reasons as to why *K'Fias Ha-Mita* has been discontinued. The *Shulchan Oruch* (*Yoreh Deah* 387:2) discusses these reasons to explain why we no longer practice this custom.

Rav Soloveitchik therefore suggests that our tradition of covering mirrors is an extension of *K'fias Ha-Mita*. Mirrors are an expression of vanity, for they serve to reflect man's image, and therefore should not be used during mourning. Furthermore, the Rav states that just as in the time of the *Gemorah* all beds in the houses of mourners had to be overturned, even those not used by the mourners, so today should all mirrors in the houses of mourners be covered, even when they're not used by the mourners themselves, such as those in guest rooms or in remote places of the house.

4

An *Aveil Kohen Duchening*

It is a mitzvahs *asei* for a *kohen* to *duchen*, upon being summoned to do so by the *Sheliach Tzibbur* when he calls out K-O-H-A-N-I-M. However, he is exempt from this mitzvah if his heart and mind are not full of joy, for it is written: *Vetov Leiv Hu Yevoreich.* According to Rav Soloveitchik, the exemption is based on the word *"B'A'Ha'Vah,"* said at end of the *bracha.*

During the seven days of *aveilus*, a *kohen* certainly does not *duchen.* However, there is a dispute among *Rishonim* as to whether he can *duchen* after the seven days. According to the *Rashbo (Teshuvos HaRashbo)*, he is required to *duchen.* The *Bais Yoseph* follows this ruling (*Orach Chaim* 128:43). The *Ramo* follows the ruling of the *Mordechai* (end of *Hakorei Omeid, Megillah*) that for parents he is exempt from *duchening* all twelve months. The *Ramo* concludes with the words "*V'Chain Nohagim Bi'Medinos Ailu,*" that this is our accepted custom.

Because it is our *minhag* to *duchen* only on *Yom Tov* and on *Yom Tov* there is no *aveilus*, then why is the *kohen* exempt from *duchening*? And why does the *Rashbo* say that a *kohen* is required to *duchen* if he also admits to the need for *Simcha Vetov Leiv* as a requirement for *duchening*?

According to Rav Soloveitchik, the difference of opinion is whether it is the absence of *tzaar* (sorrow) or the internalization of *simcha* as the prerequisite for *duchening*. According to the *Rashbo*, a *kohen* should *duchen* after the shiva period because the *tzaar* has diminished, particularly on *Yom Tov*, when there is no external observance of *aveilus*. According to the *Mordechai*, internal feelings cannot be adjusted so easily and true *simcha* cannot be felt; therefore, he does not *duchen*.

This dispute carries over to a *kohen* who never married. *Chazal* tell us that one without a wife is without *simcha*. Therefore, here, too, the *Bais Yoseph* rules that an unmarried *kohen* may *duchen* (*Orach Chaim* 128:44), while the *Ramo* quotes the opinion of the *Mordechai* against *duchening*. However, here the *Ramo* adds that a custom that an unmarried *kohen* does *duchen* has been established. Although he is not in a full capacity of *simcha* because he is without a wife, he is not necessarily in *tzaar* either.

5

An *Aveil* as *Sheliach Tzibbur* for *Maariv* on Rosh Chodesh

It is a common practice in many communities to allow a mourner to daven for the *amud* on Rosh Chodesh for *Maariv*, and even for *Shacharis* up to *Hallel*. For until *Hallel* in *Shacharis* (except for *Yaaleh Ve'Yovo*), it is considered a weekday davening.

According to Rav Soloveitchik, this is an incorrect consideration. Based upon the *Gemorah* (*Zevachim* 91a), it is quite clear that the Rosh Chodesh aspect permeates the entire day. The *Gemorah* wants to explore whether "frequency" (*taddir*) takes precedence over *kedusha*. For example, Rabbi Yochanan states that on Shabbos one should daven *Mincha* first and then *Mussof* if it is past *Chatzos*. The *Gemara* says that perhaps the *kedusha* of *Mussof*—because it is exclusively for Shabbos, whereas *Mincha* is davened daily—should take precedence over *Mincha*, which has the aspect of *taddir*. The *Gemorah*, however, rejects this inference: *Atu Shabbos Li'Tefillas Mussofim a'Hani, Li'Tefillas Mincha Lo A'Hani?* (Does the *kedusha* of Shabbos benefit only the *tefillah* of *Mussof* but not *Mincha*?) Certainly not!! Likewise, the Rov argued, the *kedusha* of Rosh Chodesh permeates the entire day and all *tefillos*, including *Maariv* and *Mincha*. Hence, an *aveil* does not daven for the *amud* for any *tefillos* of Rosh Chodesh.

6

An *Aveil Kohen* in a Funeral Chapel and Cemetery

According to Rav Soloveitchik, the question concerning whether a *kohen* in a funeral chapel or cemetery for the burial of an immediate family member can visit other *k'vorim* is a dispute between the *Meseches Sofrim* and the *Toras Kohanim*. The *Rambam paskans* like the *Toras Kohanim* and prohibits the *kohen* to visit other graves. The *Rambam* says (*Aveil* 2:15): *Lefikoch Asur L'Kohen L'Histamei L'Mais Afilu B'Ais She'Mistamie L'Krovov, She'Ne'Emar, Loh Yitamoh* (*Emor 21:3*). *Lefikoch Kohen She'Mais Tzorich L'Kovro B'Sohf Bais Hakvoros.* It is forbidden for a *kohen* to defile himself for another *mais* while he is defiling himself for his immediate relative, as it states in the Torah: "To Her May He Defile Himself"—to her, and not to any other. Therefore, a *kohen* who dies should be buried at the edge of the cemetery.

The *Mechaber* (*Yoreh Deah* 373:7) follows this ruling. However, the *Ramo* adds: *B'Ohd She'Hu Oseik B'Maiso Mutar Litamohs Af L'Acheirim*. While he is involved with his own relative, he may defile himself for others.

Therefore, Rav Soloveitchik says that a *kohen* may enter a chapel for his relative even if other funerals are taking place within the same chapel. It would be advisable, however, for the *kohen* to sit in the hearse, if possible, while driving into the cemetery so that he is directly involved in the burial of his own relative while passing through other *k'vorim*.

Part VI

Fast Days

1

The Difference Between Taanit Esther and Other Fasts

The *Rambam* (*Taanis* 5:19) says that all fast days (i.e., seventeenth of *Tammuz*, ninth of *Av*, third of *Tishre*, and tenth of *Teves*) will end in the days of *Moshiach*. Furthermore, they will become joyous holidays. He does not, however, mention Taanit Esther. Elsewhere (*Hilchos Megillah* 2:18) the *Rambam* writes that in days of *Moshiach*, all memories of past *tzoros* will be eliminated. But the days of Purim never will be eliminated.

The *Ran* (second *Perek* of *Taanis*) asks why *Chazal* instituted a *Taanis* on the thirteenth of *Adar*, before the nullification of *Megillas Taanis*, because it was prohibited to fast on the day before or after a *Yom Tov*. He answers that Taanit Esther is different from other fast days: *D'Zichron Hu L'Nais She'Na'Aseh Bo, She'K'Shem Shekiblu Aleihem La'Asos Yom Tov Kach Kiblu Aleihem La'Asos Ta'anis.*

Rav Soloveitchik therefore suggests that Taanit Esther is an integral part of Purim and not merely a fast day in and of itself. (This is similar to the mitzvah of eating on *Erev* Yom Kippur, which is related to Yom Kippur. Fasting the day before Purim enhances and embellishes the *nes* of Purim. Consequently, if Purim never becomes *botel*, neither will Taanit Esther.

The practical application would be that on other fast days, aside from the *issur* of eating and drinking, there is also an aspect of *aveilus*, prompting the *Rambam* to write: *Lo Yinhag Idunim B'Atzmoh* (one should not conduct himself with levity) (*Taanis* 1:14). This would not apply to Taanit Esther, which does not have the halakhic stringencies of mourning.

2

Washing One's Face on Yom Kippur and Tisha B'av

Although we observe many fast days throughout the year, only one is biblically ordained: Yom Kippur. All other public fast days are rabbinically ordained, including Tisha B'av.

Ironically, there is one Halakha pertaining to the fast day that is more stringent on Tisha B'av than on Yom Kippur.

The *Rambam* (*Hilchos Sh'visas Osor* 3:5) writes, based on the *Gemorah* (*Yoma* 78a), that one may soak a cloth on *Erev* Yom Kippur, squeeze it slightly, and apply it to his face on Yom Kippur, even though it is still damp, cold, and refreshing. The only problem with using a wet cloth is that it could lead to a violation of *s'chita* (squeezing), but in terms of *r'chitza* on Yom Kippur, there is no objection. The *Lechem Mishna* is bothered by the fact that on Tisha B'av there is no prohibition of *s'chita*, yet in *Hilchos Taanis* the *Rambam* specifically forbids using a wet cloth on one's face. So why are we more stringent on Tisha B'av than on Yom Kippur?

According to Rav Soloveitchik, the five *inuyyim* (prohibitions) observed on Yom Kippur are basically a fulfillment of a positive mitzvah of *sh'Visa*, for the *Rambam* (*Shvisas Osor* 1:5) writes: *Mitzvah Lishbos Mikol Eilu*. Therefore, using water absorbed by a cloth is not the usual manner of washing and, if not for the problem of *s'chita*, would be totally permissible. However, on Tisha B'av, the prohibition of washing stems from a Halakha of *aveilus* that prohibits any washing on the body that brings pleasure to a person.

3

Fast Days and Pregnant Women

The *Shulchon Oruch* (*Orach Chaim* 550:1) states that on the four public fast days—Tisha B'av, *Asoro B'Teves*, seventeenth of *Tammuz*, and *Tzom G'Dalia*—everyone is required to fast. The *Ramo* notes that on the latter three, pregnant (as well as nursing) women are exempt, even if they are not suffering. But the more stringent custom—that they fast if they are able to—prevails. On Tisha B'av, however, they are required to fast.

According to Rav Soloveitchik, the reason for the exemption on these three days is because when a pregnant woman fasts, she not only deprives herself of food, she deprives her fetus of nourishment, and the fetus definitely is not required to fast. The *Shulchon*

Oruch specifically states (554:5) that when she does eat on the three public fast days, she must limit her consumption to *K'Dai Kiyyum Ha-V'Lad* (only to satisfy the needs of her fetus). The question that arises is why should Tisha B'av be any different, for here, too, there is no obligation for the fetus to suffer.

The Rav explains that the halakhic term of *Taanis Tzibbur* applies only to Tisha B'av and not to the other three fast days—*Ain Taanis Tzibbur B'Bovel Elah Tisha B'Av Bilvad* (In the Diaspora, there are no public fast days [with the status of a 'public fast day'] except for *Tisha B'av*) (*Taanis* 11b). A *Taanis Tzibbur*, which embraces the collective body of the community of Israel, mandates by definition that the fast begin the night before and other restrictions apply. By precluding these restrictions and beginning the fast in the morning rather than the previous night, our sages were teaching us that the three fast days are in the category of a *Taanis Yochid*, where it nevertheless is incumbent upon every individual to participate.

With this in mind, we readily can understand why a fetus, as an individual, certainly is not required to participate in a *Taanis Yochid*. However, the status of the fetus is no different from that of any other member of the collective total as far as being part of the *tzibbur*. Thus, if she is able to, the mother is required to fast on Tisha B'av.

Part VII

The Wedding Ceremony

1

Placing Ashes on the Head of the *Chosson*

There are many *minhagim* observed at a wedding ceremony. Each has its own origin and should be observed according to family custom. There is one *minhag* that has its origin in talmudic sources and therefore should be treated on a different level.

The *Gemorah* (*Bava Basra* 60b), which discusses the traumatic experience of the destruction of the Holy Temple, states that Rabbi Yitzchok instructs us to remember Jerusalem at every wedding ceremony by placing burned ashes upon the *chosson*'s head. He bases this practice on the verse from Psalms 137:6: *Im Esh'Ka'Chech Yerushalayim . . . Im Loh A'Aleh Es Yerushalayim Al Rosh Simchosi* (If I forget thee, O Jerusalem . . . if I set not Jerusalem above my chief joy). The *Shulchon Oruch* (*Orach Chaim* 560:2) codifies this practice in Halakha by specifying where the ashes should be placed upon the *chosson*'s head. *B'Mokom Hanochas T'Fillin* (the area where *tefillin* are placed).

Rav Soloveitchik was always meticulous about this observance. As a matter of fact, he insisted that the ashes be placed on the *chosson*'s head under the *chuppah*, following the *Birchas Erussin* and the placement of the ring on the *kallah*'s finger. Rav Soloveitchik reasoned that the term "*chosson*" only applies to the groom after the kiddushin has taken place. Prior to *Birchas Erussin*, the groom is not halakhically identified as a *chosson* and would not satisfy the talmudic requirement.

2

The *Badecken* Ceremony Requiring Two Witnesses

Prior to the *chuppah* ceremony at a wedding, the groom joyfully is escorted to the bride with singing and dancing. When he reaches the bride, he lowers the veil over her face, having made sure that she is his intended.

According to some opinions, this custom has its origin in the story of Yitzchok and Rivkah. When Rivkah is introduced to Yitzchok for the first time, the Torah states: *Va'Ti'Kach Ha'Tzo'If Va'Tis'Kos* (Gen. 24:65) (She then took her veil and covered herself). Most opinions find the roots of this custom in the story of Yaakov, who was not permitted to view his bride's face before the wedding ceremony and was fooled into marrying Leah instead of Rachel, the woman he loved. By covering his bride's face with a veil, the groom is sure that she is the chosen one and he thereby sets her apart from all others.

Halakhically speaking, the marriage consists of two aspects: kiddushin and *nissuin*. Kiddushin is clearly defined in the *Gemorah kiddushin*: when the groom gives the bride a ring (or anything equivalent) and she willingly accepts it in front of two viable witnesses, the kiddushin is consummated. However, the *Gemorah* leaves the *nissuin* in ambiguous terms. Hence, the *Rishonim* debate the issue as to what exactly is *nissuin*.

The *Rambam* says that *nissuin* refers to the *yichud* (the seclusion of the *chosson* and the *kallah*) following the *chuppah*. This is the *mechaber*'s opinion in *Shulchon Oruch* (*Even Ho-Ezer* 55:1). However, the *Ramo* says that *nissuin* refers to the act of standing under the canopy together. A third opinion is that of the *Taz* (*Hilchos Aveilus*), who says that the *badeken* ceremony is indeed the *nissuin*.

Consequently, the *Bais Shmuel* concludes (*Even Ho-Ezer*, note 5) that we are to comply with all three opinions and conduct all three ceremonies.

Rav Soloveitchik therefore suggests a novel approach. Just as we are meticulous in designating two kosher witnesses for the kiddushin under the *chuppah*, as well as two for the *yichud* following the *chuppah*, we also must designate two to observe the *badeken* ceremony prior to the *chuppah*.

3

Fulfilling *Mesamayach Chosson V'Kallah* by Attending the Wedding's *Sheva Brochos*

One of the blessings we recite under the *chuppah* and again at the conclusion of the wedding meal includes the words *Kesameichacha Yetzircha Be'Gan Eden Mikedem*. With these words we wish that God should grant the bride and groom the happiness He bestowed upon Adam when he took Chava as his wife in *Gan Eden*.

Where do we find a source for or even a reference to the fact that *Hashem* was *Mesamayach* Adam and Chava? It is highly unlikely that *Chazal* would formulate a text for a blessing without having a specific source.

According to Rav Soloveitchik, we find in *Midrash Rabbah* (*Breishis* 8:15) the statement of Rabbi Simlai—that *Hashem* blessed the couple, for it is written: *VaYevarech Osam Elokim*, and *Hashem* blessed them (*Breishis* 1:22). The Rav comments that the blessing they received from *Hashem* is the underlying source for and the essence of *simcha*. What greater joy can we possibly experience than to be blessed by the Creator of the Universe?

The *Gemorah* (*Kesuvos* 17a) tells us that Rabbi Yehuda bar Ilai used to entertain the *kallah* by dancing in front of her with a myrtle twig and that Rav Shmuel bar Rav Yitzchok used to juggle with three myrtles to delight her. However, not everyone is capable of accomplishing such acrobatic feats. The basic fulfillment (*kiyyum*) of *simcha* is the blessing and the good wishes that each of us expresses to the *chosson* and *kallah*.

As a matter of fact, Reb Chaim Soloveitchik commented on the statement *Kol Haneheneh Mi'seudas Chassan Ve'eino Mesamaycho oveir bechamesh Kolos* (Whoever partakes of a chosson's wedding meal and does not offer him joy is in violation of five transgressions) (*Brachos* 5b). The *Gemorah* means that whoever eats at the wedding *seuda* but does not stay to take part in *sheva brachos* has failed to fulfill the precept of *Mesamayach Chosson V'Kallah*.

Part VIII

Bris Milah

1

Bris Milah Through a Nonobsdervant Mohel

The *Gemorah* (*Avoda Zora* 27a) raises the issue of a circumcision performed by a Gentile. According to Rabbi Meir, the circumcision would be recognized as valid. Rabbi Yehudi disagrees and invalidates such a bris milah. The *Gemorah* then records a dispute between the *Amoraim Rav* and *Shmuel* as to whether we follow the opinion of Rabbi Meir or Rabbi Yehuda.

The *Rambam* (*Hilchos Milah* 2:1) rules that an *Akum* (Gentile) should not perform the bris but that if he did, it is valid. The *Shulchan Aruch* (*Milah* 264:1) follows this opinion. However, the *Ramo* rules that the bris is invalid and requires a *HaTofas Dam Bris* (a token act of drawing a drop of blood).

Rabbi Akiva Eiger finds difficulty with Rabbi Meir's view, for the mohel represents the father and a Gentile cannot qualify as a *"sheliach."* So Rabbi Akiva Eiger postulates that apparently the Torah did not obligate a father to perform the bris on his child; the Torah only commissioned him to see to it that his child is circumcised. The *Shach* (*Choshen Mishpat* 382:4) disagrees and states that if he's capable, a father must fulfill the mitzvah himself and consider it a *Mitzvah Sh'B'gufoh*.

The *Ramo* adds that a nonobservant mohel (a *mumer*) has the same status as a Gentile. Consequently, his performance would be considered invalid. Several *poskim* disagree with this ruling, including the *G'Ra* and Rabbi Akiva Eiger.

Rav Soloveitchik states that this question requires subjectivity. If we are dealing with parents committed *shomrei* Torah, then we must follow the *Ramo*'s stringent ruling and not permit a nonobservant mohel to circumcise the child. However, if the parents themselves are not committed to Torah *u'mitzvos* and a religious mohel is not available on the eighth day or in the immediate future, then rather than risk the possibility of parents refusing to have the child circumcised at all—the older he gets the more difficult the bris becomes—Rav Soloveitchik allows the nonreligious mohel (doctor) to perform the bris.

2

Zeh Godole Ha-Koton Yi'H'Yeh

Immediately following the circumcision at a bris milah, the two blessings of *Krias Hashem* (name giving) are recited. In the second *bracha* of *Elokeinu Vailokei Avohseinu,* in which we beseech *Hashem* to preserve this child for his father and mother and announce the actual name to be given, the one who is reciting concludes with a wish on behalf of all those present: *Zeh Godole Ha-Koton Yi'H'Yeh* (May this little one become great).

What exactly did our sages have in mind with this concluding statement? One hardly believes that the statement refers to physical growth. Yet it is incumbent upon us to be knowledgeable of the *bracha*'s meaning.

According to Rav Soloveitchik, we must analyze the meaning of *koton* and *godole* by the context in which these terms appear in the Torah. The first time we encounter them is in *Braishis* 1:16: *Va'Ya'As . . . Ea Ha'Maore Ha-Godole L'Memsheles Ha'Yom, V'es Ha'Maor Ha-Koton L'Memsheles Ha-Lyloh* (And *Hashem* made the two great luminaries, the greater luminary to rule the day and the lesser luminary to rule the night). Thus, *godole* refers to the sun and *koton* to the moon. The moon has no light source of its own; it merely reflects what it receives from the sun. A *koton* receives, while a *godole* gives. In Torah learning the *koton* absorbs knowledge from his rebbe, his teacher, and the rebbe imparts his wisdom to his disciples.

Rav Soloveitchik explains that this is precisely what the *bracha* intends. This child, who is now a *koton*, a receiver, should develop into a *godole* who someday will illuminate the wisdom of Torah for others.

3

Burying a Noncircumcised Child in a Jewish Cemetery

The *Mechaber* (*Yorah Deah* 263:5) quotes the opinion of some *Geonim* that if a child dies without having been circumcised, Halakha requires that a bris milah be performed prior to burial. To underscore the seriousness of this Halakha, the *Pischai Teshuva* (note 11) quotes a dispute among *Acharonim* (*Nodeh Bi'y'huda*) about whether the grave should be opened in the event the bris was not performed.

In a situation where the parents are not *shomrei* Torah *u'Mitzvos* and refuse permission for such a circumcision, may the child be buried in a Jewish cemetery?

According to Rav Soloveitchik, the *Chevra* kaddisha should not withhold permission for such a burial. The Rav explains that the common belief that a bris milah is for *machen ihm a Yid* (to make him Jewish) is absolutely incorrect. In the case of a convert, the bris milah is an integral part of the conversion process. It elevates him unto *kedushas Yisroel*. Regarding a child born to a Jewish mother, the circumcision is strictly for the mitzvah, but not for conversion, for the child is born Jewish in every aspect. The *Gemorah* (*Chulin* 5a) specifically states: *Hakol Shochatim, Afilu Orail* (We validate the *Sh'chita* of a noncircumcised Jew and regard him as Jewish even if his neglect of a bris was out of choice rather than out of ill health).

Rav Soloveitchik further notes that this question arose in Warsaw more than ninety years ago and that his grandfather, Reb Chaim, also ruled that way and brought many other sources to support his opinion.

Part IX

Teshuva

1

Suicide as a Form of *Teshuva*

The Torah (*Parshas Noach* 9:5) teaches: *V'Ach Es Dim'Chem L'Naf'Sho'Seichem Ed'Rosh* (However, your blood which belongs to your souls I will demand). *Chazal* learn from here the prohibition of self-murder, or suicide (see *Rashi*).

The *Rambam* (*Hilchos Rotzeiach* 2:2) considers this a severe prohibition and writes: *Ha-Horeig Es Atzmo Chayov Misoh La-Shomayim* (One who commits suicide is punishable as a murderer by *Hashem*). However, one who murders another person is punishable by *Bais Din*. The *Minchas Chinuch* suggests a practical difference between the two. In accordance with the principle of *Kom Leh Mideraba Mineh*, anyone sentenced by *Bais Din* to be executed for murder would be exempt from any monetary damages. *Misah Bidei Shomayim*, however, does not allow such an exemption.

In the case of the suicide, we deem the perpetrator as a *rasha* and deprive him the honors of a eulogy. And no shiva is observed, unless we ascertain medical or mental reasons for his behavior.

If the suicide was for a noble purpose—for example, if someone feels such remorse over a terrible sin that he goes beyond the level of *teshuva* (repentance) and feels compelled to inflict upon himself the supreme punishment of death—is this person regarded as a *tzaddik* or a *rasha*? The *Gemorah* (*Avoda Zora* 17a) relates the story of Rabbi Elazer ben Durdaya, who, after a lifetime of sin, suddenly was inspired to repent. When it became painfully clear to him that no one would help him and his repentance depended solely upon himself, he placed his head between his knees and wept until his soul departed. A *Bas Kol* then emerged from on high, proclaiming that Elazer ben Durdaya was prepared to enter directly into *Olam Haboh*.

According to Rav Soloveitchik, it is indeed a sin for one to cause his own death—even if for *teshuva* purposes. He says that our *Gemorah* cannot be cited as proof that it is halakhically sanctioned because it does not say that Elazer ben Durdaya directly caused his own death. It is possible that he just died from intense pain and remorse but did not actually kill himself.

However, the Rav notes that even if we cannot sanction such an extreme course of *teshuva*, a person who nevertheless is overzealous in his quest for penitence and takes his own life is not treated as a *rasha* and sinner but is to be honored as a *tzaddik* with a proper eulogy and mourning (*Birkei Yosef, Yora Deah* 345:2).

2

Seeking Forgiveness Before Yom Kippur

The *Mishna* (*Bava Kama* 92a) states that in a case of injury to his fellow man, even if the perpetrator compensates the injured party with all monetary expenses—*nezek, tzaar, ripue, sheves,* and *boshes*—he is not forgiven until he formally requests forgiveness. This is based on the *posuk* (*Braishis* 20:7) *Veatoh Hoshaiv Aishes Ho'ish Ki Novie Hu, Vyispallel Ba'Ad'cha,* which indicates that Avimelech was not forgiven until he begged forgiveness from Avraham so that Avraham will pray for him.

The *Mishna* (*Yoma* 85b) states that *aveiros* (sins) between man and *Hashem—Yom Kippur* effects atonement. But *aveiros* between man and fellow man Yom Kippur will not effect atonement until he pacifies his friend. Rabbi Elazar Ben Azariah bases this on the *posuk* (*Vayikro 16:30*) *Mikol Chatosaichem Lifnai Hashem Tithoru.*

Why is there a need for Rabbi Elazar Ben Azariah's d'rosho when we already have a *posuk* in *Braishis* quoted in *Bava Kama?*

Rav Soloveitchik suggests that there are two aspects to forgiveness. In all year-round confrontations, merely pacifying an injured friend is sufficient. That is what the *Mishna* in *Bava Kama* states. However, before Yom Kippur, ordinary appeasement is not enough. *We are required to seek a restored relationship, to enjoy once again the kind of deep and trusting friendship we enjoyed before our misunderstanding occurred.* That is what the *Rambam* refers to in *Hilchos Teshuva* 2:9. Even though he returns the money he owes, *Tzorich Lratzoso Ulishol Mimenu Sheyimchol Lo* (He must restore his relationship with him, and seek his forgiveness). Two things are needed: forgiveness through appeasement (*limchol lo*) and a restored relationship (*l'ratzoso*).

Part X

Miscellaneous Questions

1

Discarding Old, Worn-Out *Tzitzis*

The *Gemorah* (*Megillah* 26b) states: *Tashmishei Mitz-vah Nizrakin, Tashmishei Kedusha Nignazin.* Objects once used in the performance of a mitzvah that has now ended—e.g., a *lulav* after Sukkos or *tzitzis* on a *tallis* that have worn out—are examples of *tashmishei* mitzvah that can be *nizrakin* (simply discarded). However, *tashmishei kedusha* (objects of intrinsic *kedusha*)—e.g., *tefillin* or a *Sefer* Torah—that are worn out (*nignazin*) must be buried.

It appears from this *Gemorah* that *tzitzis*, though used in the performance of a mitzvah, are indeed objects of a mitzvah but are not regarded as *dovor kedusha*, and therefore may be discarded, even in garbage, when no longer needed or usable as a mitzvah.

That is precisely how the *Mechaber* (*Orach Chaim* 21:1) rules. However, the *Ramo* cites the *Kol Bo*, who says that while *tzitzis* do not require *geniza* (burial), they should not be disposed of in the garbage. This would be a *bizayon* (disgrace) to them. Rav Moshe Feinstein, zt"l, suggests wrapping the *lulav* (after Sukkos) or worn-out *tzitzis* in separate newspapers and then placing them on top of the garbage as a viable solution. The *Ramo* then adds that those punctilious in observing mitzvos should place them into *geniza*. The *Mishne Berura* cites the *Maharil*, who suggests using the *tzitzis* as a bookmark in a *Sefer* or for some other *d'var* mitzvah.

According to Rav Soloveitchik, the premise that *tefillin* have intrinsic *kedusha* while *tzitzis* do not enables us to understand another Halakha based on this concept. When it becomes necessary to go to the bathroom while davening, we remove our *tallis* and *tefillin*. Upon returning to daven, we again put them on; the *tefillin* require another *bracha*, while the *tallis* does not, even though there was no *hesech hadaas* for either one. Why? Because *tefillin* have *kedusha* and thus are prohibited from being brought into the bathroom. This prohibition creates an automatic case of *hesech hadaas*. However, the *tallis*, having no *kedusha*, technically may be permitted into the bathroom. The fact that we remove it before entering is not *m'ikar HaDin*, but only a sign of *kavod* for *tallis*; the *tallis koton* underneath the shirt is not removed (because it is not visible). Therefore, because this is not a *hesech hadaas* situation, there is no need for another *bracha*.

2

Washing for Food Dipped in Liquid

The *Gemorah* (*Pesachim* 115a) states that any food dipped in liquid requires washing: *N'Tilas Yodayim*. According to *Tosfos*, this practice was only applicable in the days of the *Bais Hamikdash* because *Stam Yodayim Shniyos* (in general, hands are regarded as a secondary degree of impurity) and a *sheni* is *Oseh Shlishi* (upon contact, an item of a secondary degree of impurity will cause *Terumah* [the first portion of the crop that is separated and given to a *Kohen*] to become a third degree of impurity) to *terumah*. There was indeed a rabbinic ruling that whatever causes a *psul* in *terumah* requires washing of the hands. (This was one of the eighteen decrees of the rabbis mentioned in first *perek* of *Gemorah* Shabbos). Therefore, *Tosfos* concludes that washing is no longer necessary today.

Rav Soloveitchik, basing his opinion on his interpretation of the *Rambam*, disagrees. He says that even if the original reason does not apply, it is still incumbent upon us even today to follow the *takono* of the rabbis and wash with a *bracha* (*Rambam, Hilchos Brachos* 6:1). According to the Rav, the *Rambam* similarly holds that washing for *karpas* at the Seder should be with a *bracha* (*Hilchos Chometz Umatza* 8:1). That was the prevailing *minhag* in Brisk. The *Shulchon Oruch* (*Orach Chaim* 158:4) basically agrees with the *Rambam* and requires *n'tilas yodayim* all year whenever food is dipped in liquid. But no *bracha* is made because of *Tosfos*'s opinion. Similarly, the *Mechaber* rules that we wash for *karpas* at the Seder but without a *bracha* (ibid 473:6).

The *Gra* also rules totally in favor of the *Rambam* and personally washed with a *bracha* at the Seder, as well as all year round when he dipped his cake into coffee.

The *Mogen Avraham* comments, in the name of the *Lechem Chamudos*, that the prevailing *minhag* is not to wash at all. The *Mishne Brura*, however, feels that we should wash today whenever we dunk our doughnuts, but without a *bracha*.

The *Taz* asks that if the prevailing custom is not to wash, then why do we wash for *karpas* at the

Seder? The *N'Tziv* answers in his *Hagadah* that it's not because of a *chumra*, but rather because it's a *zaicher l'mikdash*. Therefore, he cites the *Maharil* that the *minhag* was only for the father to wash at the Seder, but not the other participants.

3

Halakhic Considerations for Sensitive People

Rav Soloveitchik often notes that Halakha indeed makes certain accommodations for those who are extremely delicate, referred to as *istenis*.

During the seven days of *shiva*, an *aveil* is prohibited from washing and bathing. However, Rabban Gamliel did bathe himself during this period. When his students questioned his actions, he responded, "I am an *istenis*" (*Brachos* 16b). *Tosfos* comments that bathing only for pleasure is prohibited but in his case it was *tzaar*, or pain. For this reason many *poskim* permit bathing on *Erev* Shabbos *Chazone* because we are all considered *istenis* when it comes to bathing. (This applies only when an *issur* is a *minhag*.)

Regarding Yom Kippur, the *Shulchon Aruch*

(*Orach Chaim* 613:4) permits an *istenis* to wash his face under certain circumstances. The *Ramo*, however, prohibits it. According to the Rav, if it is for therapeutic reasons, it would be permissible (see also *Mishna Berura*).

Concerning leaving the Sukkah because of rain, the *Gemorah* (*Sukkah* 29a) says that it is a subjective matter. Rav Yosef and *Abbaye* were eating in the Sukkah when it began to rain. Rav Yosef immediately suggested leaving, but *Abbaye* protested that it wasn't sufficient rain to exempt them from Sukkah. Rav Yosef responded: "To me, as a sensitive person, the situation warrants leaving the Sukkah."

In *Hilchos Seuda* (*Orach Chaim* 170), there are a number of Halakhos mentioned to assure that one does not do anything to offend a sensitive person.

Rav Soloveitchik even adds that *teshuva* is required for acting insensitively toward someone, even if it's done unintentionally. Rav Yochanan (*Chagiga* 5a) wept when he read *Al Kol Ne'elam* (*Koheles* 12:14), that *Hashem* will hold us responsible even for an innocent act such as killing an insect in front of someone who is sensitive about it. It isn't enough to follow the rule of *Hillel*: "What is hateful to you, do not do to your friend" (*Shabbos* 31a). This would imply that if it doesn't bother you, you can do it to your friend. This is not true, for Halakha requires us to consider the sensitivity of others as well.

4

Defining *Lifnei Eevair*

According to Rav Soloveitchik, *Chazal* have interpreted this *posuk* (*Kedoshim* 19:14) in many ways. It cautions us against any careless word or act that in any manner could endanger the material or moral welfare of another. The term "blind man" refers not to one who is physically blind, but to one who is intellectually or morally "blind" or "blinded" by strong emotions. The specific interpretations can be found in *Psachim 22b*, *Moed Katan 5a* and *17a*, *Kiddushim 32a*, *Nedarim 62b*, *Bava Metzia 75a*, *Chulin 75a*, and *Avoda Zara 14a*.

What if one actually were to place a rock in the path of one who cannot see? Would he be in violation of *Lifnei Eevair*? Rav Soloveitchik states that at first glance, the answer is definitely yes. However, we note from the *Rambam* and the *Chinuch* (*Mitzvah* 232) that it is not so. The *Chinuch* states that this mitzvah does not carry the punishment of *malkos* because it is a "*Lav Sh'Ain Bo Maaseh*," it is entirely passive without any physical action being done. Why is placing a stone in front of someone who cannot see considered a *Lav Sh'Ain Bo Maaseh*? The Rav surmises that apparently the *Chinuch* considers only *Chazal*'s interpretations of *Lifnei Eevair*, but not the literal meaning of the *posuk*.

The problem with this is the statement in the *Gemorah* (*Shabbos* 62b): "*Rav Kahana* said I have been studying *Shas* for eighteen years, but only now do I realize that *Ain Mikroh Yotze Mideai P'Shuto*." We cannot ignore or deny the literal meaning of a *posuk*. (The only exception to this rule is the one about naming a firstborn after the deceased brother, in the case of *yibbum* in *Devorim* 25:6). So how can both the *Rambam* and the *Chinuch* absolutely ignore the literal meaning of this *posuk*?

According to Rav Soloveitchik, it appears that placing a stone in front of a blind person is such a grotesque, monstrous act that the Torah did not even think it worthy of mention. For a Jew to act in a manner of *achzorius* would cause us, *Chazal* say, to question his pedigree of Jewishness. And because the Torah is addressing the Jewish people, it was entirely unnecessary and thus not included.

5

The *Derech Hashem*: How to React to Difficult Situations

Halakha does not merely dictate what mitzvos we are to perform and the precise method of executing them. It also directs us in how to react to circumstances.

The *Rambam*, based on the *Gemorah* (*Sota* 5a) and other sources, devotes his entire first *perek* of *Hilchos Dai'os* to channeling our moods to the *Sh'Vil Ha-Zahav*, the Golden Rule of the middle road, the way of Torah, which is the way of *Hashem*. The *Rambam* says that this is precisely what is meant concerning *Avraham Avinu*: that he will convey this concept to his children (*L'Maam Asher Yetzaveh Es Bonov.... V'Shomru Derect Hashem La'Asos Tzedaka Umishpot*), that he will guide them to follow the way of *Hashem* to engage in righteousness and justice (Gen. 18:19).

The traditional understanding of this directive is that a person always should avoid pursuing the extreme in any given circumstance but should position himself somewhere in the middle. When confronted with a provocative situation, we must not be overly passive and do nothing, but we also dare not overreact.

Rav Soloveitchik did not believe this to be the correct interpretation of this famous cardinal rule. The Rav did not believe that *Chazal* and the *Rambam* meant that we should be perfectly predictable human beings and that in any given circumstance we should act like robots and make it obvious to all exactly how we react. The *Sh'Vil Ha-Zahav* is called the *Derech Hashem*, and the way of *Hashem* is not always predictable. At times He appears as all-merciful, while at other times He seeks revenge. *Hashem* is identified with peace, while at other times as *Ish Milchama*.

According to Rav Soloveitchik, the Golden Rule, then, is a process. We are called upon to evaluate each situation and determine if it warrants a battle cry or peace negotiations. We are not to respond in an extreme manner as the only alternative, but first must make every effort to appease before reverting to war. On occasion we are required to be generous, forgiving, and tolerant, but at other times we must demand and react appropriately. If we were to analyze our responses over the years, we would find them falling somewhere in the middle. This represents the true *Derech Hashem*.

INDEX

About the Author

Rabbi Aharon Ziegler, spiritual leader of Congregation Agudath Achim of Boro Park in Brooklyn, New York for the past thirty-five years, is a retired librarian for the New York City Board of Education. A student of the Rav for many years, Rabbi Ziegler does extensive lecturing and writing on the halakhic positions of Rabbi Joseph B. Soloveitchik.